A TRUE
UFO STORY

PERMUTATION

Shirlè Klein-Carsh

Ann Carol Ulrich

PERMUTATION

A TRUE UFO STORY

Shirlè Klein-Carsh
Ann Carol Ulrich

Earth Star Publications
Pagosa Springs, Colorado

First Edition 1993
REVISED EDITION   June 2013

ISBN 978-0-944851-37-1

Published in the United States of America

Cover Art by Shirlè Klein-Carsh

PERMUTATION

Distinguishable object or elements—each different arrangement of the elements is a permutation.

The group of all permutations of objects of order is called the symmetric group. Since the cosmos is explained in mathematics and mathematics explains our own solar system, therefore the change on our Earth from one life to another becomes permutated. The change from bad to good.

Every group is mirror to some permutation group. It is easy to find a representation of a permutation group by using a permutation matrix—each life, an existence of such a matrix, has but one element and that is *unity.*

The explanation given by the aliens

Ah, Life, Life!
your delights are few
but your lessons many

i dare say

and yet
without them
shear plod your charms

I Am
but, a plaything
in your garden of invention

just a Tom Thumb

"aye, that's the rub!"

a microcosm!
and you … ahhhh!
the macrocosm!

you cause the "macro"
i cause the "micro"

let it be known!
whatever is caused
we caused it

you
and
i

life, you are a devil
a dual thing
good and evil

lived and devil
bitter and sweet
heaven and hell

she and he
you and me

i love you Life

and yet!

to leave
to die
to sleep

ahhhh!

"miles to go before I sleep,"
sweet sleep!

i love you, Life
you are
my beloved.

Pan/10/88nm

Frank Lewis Morton

CONTACTEES WHO HAVE HAD MILITARY HARASSMENT

DV: Military personnel in woods chased him. MIBs, Sasquatch encounters. Contact.

MN: Military incarcerated him in mental asylum. "German" sounding doctor ordered 7 shots of Haldol to be administered all at once without antidote—tried to kill him. Contact.

DM: CIA worked him over and had slow poison administered to him (hemi synch can cause seizures and ever since contact he has had seizures when someone tries to put him in hypnosis). Contact. Cannot work due to nervous condition and extreme allergies which developed after contact. On government assistance (how ludicrous!).

D: Taken into underground base at Site 51—kept for 26 days —did experiments on him. Military wore black uniforms and red insignias. Put in special forces so he could not talk. Contact.

P: Hounded by military & FBI because of contact in N. Carolina. Lost everything. She and her father keep constantly on the move to keep away. Contact.

HS: Policeman in Ashland, Nebraska, held for 21 days by military under hypnosis with arm in air and needles stuck in him to ascertain if he was telling truth and really under hypnosis. He had been chased for one year. Lost everything. Contact.

MB: Followed by a Capt. Morgan. Implant that came out of nose and two artifacts given to him by aliens confiscated by military. Held by armed guard in room. Constantly on the move to keep away. Contact.

RR: FBI came to house and demanded to see files on his Soviet Parapsychology research. Contact.

JG: Policeman took pictures of aliens. Hounded—house burned down, lost job, wife left him. From Greensboro, S.C.

RR: FBI came to house and demanded to see files on his Soviet Parapsychology research. Contact.

PM: 3 attempts on life by C.I.A. Water system on ranch sabotaged and his cattle mutilated. Bank account tampered with. Lost everything. Contact.

LT: FBI harassed town of "Blue Diamond" searching for Pleiadians. Made things hot for L., so he moved. Knows lots of cases of military harassment.

BJ: Abducted on military and Indian reservation near underground base site.

DP: In Metro Mall—Phoenix, AZ—taken by a "security guard" to his office in basement. Saw a picture of herself on wall. Let her go. Asked if she knew anyone else on wall! Contact.

CS: Contact. Harassed by Army to retire. Refused. Worked on "Project Snowbird" research for last 3 years.

AR: ELF wave beamed at her house (or something akin to it). Made her husband and herself sick and her teeth started turning brown. This happened after they became involved in the "Psychotronics" organization. Contact.

WR: On military plane en route to Europe. Hit by "lightning" (plane lit up). Next thing he remembers he was on step of barracks. Many gaps in memory—felt he was drugged. Next on a farm where everyone laughed. Next in a hospital in South Africa. From there sent to N.Y., where he was incarcerated in "mental" hospital with people who had "big" heads and looked strange. Said they squeaked. They were kept behind a fence from him. Psychiatrist wanted to know what he was doing there, that there was nothing wrong with him. Let him go. Now has seizures and a nervous condition that prevents him from working. On assistance.

CONTENTS

Chapter 1

Early Encounters

The shop was trashy. It wasn't the kind of store you'd want to go into. There was junk lying around and, for that matter, it didn't look clean.

"You really want to go inside *there?*" Mike asked me.

"Look, if you won't take me in, I'll go by myself." I stepped out of the car and headed for the shop. I could hear Mike grumbling as he slammed the car door and followed me.

I really didn't notice the man inside the shop right away. He sort of blended in with the interior. He was a man who looked to be in his late or mid forties. He had long black hair and a sallow or light brown complexion. He wore light brown, baggy pants and a shirt.

"Hmph," Mike grunted as he brushed past me.

I walked around and wondered to myself, "What am I doing here?"

Mike walked over to the man in the shop and started talking to him. Apparently the man was busy doing some mathematical equations and Mike was immediately interested.

"Oh ... my ... what is it you're doing there? What are all these equations?"

The man turned to Mike and said, "It's not of this world."

Overhearing his remark, I slapped my cheek as I thought to myself, "Dear God, a nut!" But when I looked up, the man turned to me. He had huge, saucer-shaped eyes that looked black from where I stood. He looked right at me and he smiled. I knew he had read my mind. Later I would discover that I had met my contact.

Most my life I lived in Montreal. My mother, father, two sisters, one brother and I lived in a typical Jewish surrounding. At the tender age of 3 my mother decided I should take piano lessons. She remembered a message she had been given on the day I was born:

That day was June 13, 19__. My mother lay in a hospital labor room in Montreal. The nurses came in and out, but my mother paid no attention. She was in agony—a young Polish woman far from her home who was getting ready to give birth to her first child.

Her name was Bella Edelstein. She and her husband Meyer, my father, had been married a year and had immigrated to Canada from Poland. Through her suffering she thought of her homeland and wished she had never come to this country and gotten married. No one had warned her what it would be like. No one had told her there would be so much pain.

Suddenly, before her eyes, my mother saw an angel appear. She *thought* it was an angel. It had to be. What else could it be? It was true there were no wings, and yet here in front of her was this magnificent being of light.

"Bella," the angel called to her. "Bella, listen to me. I have something to tell you."

My mother cringed as she felt another contraction grip her bulging middle. She cried out, this time more from fear than from pain, and when the tightness subsided, the angel held out a glass of orange juice.

"Here, drink this," it said to her, "it will make you feel better."

My mother somehow believed the angel and accepted the glass of orange juice. As she drank it slowly, she heard the angel speak in an urgent voice.

"The child you are carrying is very special, Bella. This child will someday be very famous and is indeed a special child."

My mother looked into the glass which was now half empty. It certainly felt and tasted like orange juice. She drank the rest. Immediately she felt relief and settled back, closing her eyes. When she looked again, the angel had vanished. The empty orange juice glass was on the table beside her.

Very soon afterwards, I was born. Meyer and Bella gave me the name Sarah and my mother remembered the angel's visit and wondered what my life would be like.

And so, remembering what the angelic being had told her, my mother thought I should have piano lessons as soon as possible. To my mother, playing the piano and becoming an accomplished musician was the height of being famous.

However, I rejected her plans of making me into a child prodigy. I just wasn't meant for that. Partially as a result, my childhood was a rather unhappy one. I felt as though I could never find my place. I was never really a part of anything going on around me. The things I participated in consisted more of my standing aside from it all. I remember someone telling me once, "You have the saddest eyes." It was true. I was unhappy much of the time because I simply wasn't in my place. I was always searching.

Because my mother was a very psychic person, I had many things happen to me. For instance, when I was a little girl, I once told my younger sister, "Mary, let's not walk on the grass."

"Why, Sarah? What's wrong with the grass?"

"Nothing. Let's just not walk on it because it hurts the grass if you walk on it."

My sister told me, "Don't say that! People will be very frightened of what you said."

I often talked that way. Frequently I would know what was going to happen before it actually happened.

Once I told my parents they weren't my real parents. I got smacked good for that and spent the whole day up in my room. I was given no food because of what I had said, and yet I couldn't help it. I suppose part of it was because of being the firstborn. There was no question that I was a rebellious child.

Throughout my early childhood I went by my given name—Sarah. However, I exchanged the name of Sarah for Shirlè when I started going to school. In class, when the teacher would call on Sarah, about seven of us would answer. So one day the teacher put some names on the board and one of them was Shirley. I then went home and asked my parents if I could have that name. Of course they weren't thrilled about it. But I told them I was going to have that name anyway. Later on in life I changed the name to Shirlè.

I did well in school. There was always somebody somewhere willing to help me when I got stuck. I always had helpers when there was a problem in arithmetic and math or whatever. Even as a child I was constantly searching for new knowledge.

"Shirlè, you'd better watch it," my mother told me. "You are getting too smart. You will never get married because if you're too smart, men aren't even going to look at you twice." She was of the Jewish influence that believed men did not want to marry smart girls or smart women. But it didn't matter to me. I felt I had to know what was going on around me because I felt like a stranger in a strange land.

When I got to high school, I took a commercial background, against my will, for the simple reason that my mother didn't want me to starve. At the time I wanted to be a scientist, or an artist … and my mother almost had a fit.

Once a teacher in my high school sent me home with a letter that said I had so much artistic talent that he thought I should take art lessons. He practically begged my mother to please let me develop my artistic skills. My mother tore up the letter and said, "Never! Artists always starve." What she didn't understand was that when the gift is within you, it cannot be knocked out of you. But I went into commercial and graduated, and it did help me later in life, when I had to work in an office to support myself.

My life actually started to evolve when I met my first husband, who turned out to be my first guide, or so I have been told. I was taking a walk in the country one day, and as I was coming down a hill, there was Hymie Klein, sitting in a boat with his brothers. Later I found out that he told his brothers, "See that girl walking down that hill? That's the girl I'm going to marry." They laughed at him and said, "You haven't even spoken to her yet."

When Hyman Klein first began to pursue me, I wanted nothing to do with him—and the more he tried to pursue me, the more I resisted him—until, of course, I finally got to know him.

Hymie knew such things! I would love to listen to him talk. I couldn't believe the many things that he knew. I learned so much from him. Hymie was older than me by a year and a half, but he was so wise. He was my soulmate and he was extremely wise.

These things were confirmed to me later by my contact, as I will explain. Later I was also to learn that Hymie actually helped to raise my consciousness from the other side. I required a lot of help, believe me, from all aspects. Hymie was in contact with my alien friend. Together they worked on various things.

After we were married a few short years, Hymie convinced me to go back to school, since I only had a high school degree. By that time we already had two small children, yet he encouraged me to enroll at the university. Of course, my even thinking of going to the university at that time was unheard of in those days. A lot of people made fun of me. Some people spread gossip about my marriage not working, that I was looking for other things. It was all a lack of understanding on their part.

Hymie even gave me art lessons and instruction in elocution. I performed in plays and, through art lessons, I discovered I had tremendous talent, which was latent due to the fact that my parents never wanted me to be an artist. As a matter of fact, one teacher asked me to move in with her. When I asked her for how long it would be, she said one year. Well, I had no intention of leaving my home, Hymie and the children, so I chose the "long road," so to speak, and ten years later I did make it as an artist.

It seems that wherever I've gone I've been the first at everything. I am always breaking ground. There are certain people who are adaptable at breaking ground, and I think I am one of them. Once I break ground and it's done, and other people are working on it, then I know that it's time for me to move on. This goes for everything in my life. So, in addition to being a wife and mother, who is going to college, I had to contend with people around me who disapproved of what I was doing.

I would leave the dinner and taking care of the kids to my husband while I went to school. Then I would come home and study at night. When exam time came around, I was bothered because I had so much to study for and it was difficult to find the time to get everything done.

But I had help. I hate to admit this, but the only reason I got through the university was because I had a voice inside me, telling me exactly what I needed to study to pass my exams. I would flip the pages because I was told "flip the pages" and I was shown what would be on the exam. This is how I went to school. I didn't have to study everything. I only studied what they told me I had to study, and that way I found school a lot easier.

The voice inside of me has always been with me, but when I was at the university the voice became more prominent. I was guided in many instances. Once the voice told me, "Don't go in there," like I was being protected from harm, and I would heed the warning. I took it as a natural thing. I didn't make anything out of it because I wasn't into the idea that it was something different or unusual. That thought never occurred to me. It was all simply a part of me.

Once when I was going somewhere to a party with a group of girls, the voice said to me, "Shirlè, stay home." And then I found out that other things happened. At the time, though, I didn't attach anything to it. Whatever happened, I didn't attach any importance to it until much later on. Often instead of the voice I would just get a strong feeling. However, I sometimes have a habit of not listening. If I wouldn't abide by the feeling, then I would get the voice, for emphasis.

One night while I was at home studying, I saw two people appear in front of me. They were dressed in wet suit gear, complete with flippers, and they had tanks on their backs. From the very first I associated them with space people, but I don't know why I did. From all aspects they resembled scuba divers, but somehow I knew they were space people. They both looked at me and one of them said to the other, "Shall we take her?" I could hear the conversation in my head. Then they looked really hard at me and one said, "No, not yet." And that was it.

The weird thing is I found myself in bed, facing the other way. In other words, I had started out with my head at the headboard, but suddenly I was turned around with my head at the footboard. One minute I had been studying, and suddenly ... what was I doing *here*? At the time I did not realize that I had had an episode of missing time. Many years later, under hypnotic regression, I was able to relive this experience, which is recorded in detail in a subsequent chapter.

After that encounter I became more aware. I went searching in all the libraries and second hand bookstores. At that time, either 1958 or 1962, it was very difficult to get UFO books. I really tried. My first literary contact was with George Adamski, and that helped me a great deal.

I would look through the newspaper and when there were some meetings, I would go. I had the chance to meet with some scientists, and I learned that the space people were helping a great deal in the space program. I was very pleased to hear about that. Hymie went with me to these meetings. He took part in everything that I did. He was quite supportive.

On another occasion, while I was still in college, I had another visitation, this time by a strange lady. I remember I was studying for an exam the next day, and I was thoroughly fed

The Woman From Out of the Past

up with everything that was going on in my life. I was fed up because my parents were giving me a difficult time, for one thing. God love them, my parents were hard on me. I realize now why this was so. I was such a sensitive individual. If they had gone along with me all those years, I would have been too sensitive to take the hard road that followed.

My parents and I just didn't see eye to eye on anything. If I said it was black, they said it was white. There just wasn't anything we could congeal in any way. The important thing is I learned from that, and somehow they strengthened me a tremendous amount. I now appreciate that. I realize it was all for my benefit.

This particular night I was lying in bed, studying, and in walked this strange lady out of nowhere. She came over to me and she said, "Get up." She had black eyes and was dressed in ancient attire, like from something out of the past, with a bun in the back of her head and old clothes. After she told me to get up, she did an even stranger thing. She climbed into bed with me and cradled me.

Startled, I could hear the kids in the background, and I said to her, "You'd better get out of here. The kids are going to be frightened if they see you." I told her this mentally. So she smiled, then she gave me a kiss and simply disappeared. This was apparently another nuance to help me out of a slump.

In yet another instance, still while I was going to school, I had another psychic experience. I would sometimes see a veil lift, and I would sometimes see a whole landscape from my window, which was totally alien to me. It was so beautiful with the most exotic birds, just out of nowhere. It would lift, and I would see. One night as I lay in bed, again depressed because of the difficulty with my parents and the various other people making me feel like I didn't belong, I suddenly watched as the ceiling above me disappeared.

I must have astral traveled. That's the only way I can explain it. I saw the bluest blue. To this day I cannot describe that shade of blue. I've tried so hard in my art to match that color which I saw because it was absolutely the most beautiful blue I've ever seen. I have never seen anything like it again. And here was this man, sitting on a podium, and he was putting out a whole bunch of Hebrew letters.

"That's right," he said to me, "you don't understand anything here. But if you don't change your life—like this—you are going to die."

The next thing I knew, I found myself in the living room. How I ended up there instead of my bedroom, I don't know. Anyway, I walked back to bed, but that dream or whatever was so vivid—it *did* change my life. From that point on, I wasn't that hurt when my parents said things to me. I decided to give them love no matter how they treated me because they didn't understand me and I didn't understand them. My life changed after that. I began to evolve.

Chapter 2

Contact on Fourth Avenue

The years passed. Hymie and I moved to another house in Montreal. Then all of a sudden Hymie wanted to sell it. At that time my daughter was married and we just had our son living at home. Ronny was just finishing high school.

One night in 1968 Hymie had a dream that he was going to die. He was ill. Hymie was 46 years old and had hardening of the arteries. This was the time of the first heart transplants, so we thought maybe Hymie would be lucky and get one, but he developed diabetes. In his dream Hymie was told to put his house in order because they were going to take him.

He then went about doing various things I did not understand, which included selling the house. Then he got me a studio. He said to me, "What kind of an artist are you without a studio?"

Hymie then tried to teach me how to sleep alone. I have never liked sleeping alone, and Hymie knew I had to learn. He did things that nobody seemed to understand, but he said, "I'm doing it for you." In my confusion, at first I thought there might be another woman, but he said to me, "I love you so much. You're my arms, you're my legs, you're my heart. You're a part of me. I'm doing it all for you." Then he told me, "I just came back from my mother's grave, begging God that you will find somebody … because you shouldn't be alone." That's how much he loved me.

In late August of 1968, I held an art exhibit and a man by the name of Fred Herscovitch bought one of my paintings. I was surprised when he called me up a couple of weeks later and said to me, "You are searching for the truth." I didn't know what to say. He said, "I have something to tell you. Could we meet?"

Hymie and I were getting ready that day to go over to our daughter's house. It was September 19 and his birthday had been just five days ago, on September 14. Hymie said he was going to go to the bank. He said goodbye to me, told me he'd see me soon, and left. Well, I met with this man, Fred Herscovitch, who had told me he had something to tell me, and he handed me a book by Dr. Raymond Bucke, *Cosmic Consciousness*. At that very moment Hymie died. My son found him, and it was a bad time for us.

When I called Mr. Herscovitch up and told him what had happened, he said, "Yes, I know. Now I'll come over." Then he started telling me about this agni yoga group that I was supposed to join. You can't just join the agni yoga group. You have to be asked when you are ready. A New York guru by the name of Ralph Houston told Fred Herscovitch I would have to join their group. Apparently the time had come for me to join. I found that everyone else in the group was younger than I, but it didn't make any difference. When you're ready, age makes no difference.

The group leader then came to me and we had a long talk in which we discussed many things. He told me I'd be wonderful for their group, just as the group would help me. One of the best times of my life was when I belonged to the agni yoga group because I helped them and they helped me. If it hadn't been for that group, it would have taken me a much longer time to overcome what I went through in losing my husband.

I never did see the guru. Every time I was willing to go see him, something worked out that I couldn't see him. Later on I learned, through my contact, that he wasn't supposed to meet me.

During this period it seemed everybody I knew tried to fix me up with men. Some of the women were threatened by that and I lost a lot of my friends as I was very attractive. They seemed to think I would perhaps run after their husbands. It just goes to show you how ignorant they were.

I was really suffering, and I had no one I could count on. I think my sister and my brother-in-law were the only ones who really took pity on me. Mary and Leonard helped me a lot. Otherwise everybody ran away from me, and I had to do things on my own. Looking back on it now, I can see I was able to resolve a lot of karma as quickly as possible.

It wasn't more than a few months after I lost my husband that my best friend and her husband came and asked if I would loan them my inheritance from Hymie. Her husband said to me, "Loan me the money for one year. I'll take you to a notary and you'll receive X amount of the percentage." He convinced me that this would help me in the long run, that it was a sound investment. They made it sound like a good picture, and I never questioned them because I trusted these friends. So they took me to the notary and they wrote up a whole paper and everything. I didn't realize at the time that it wasn't worth the paper it was written on.

Six months to a year went by and everything was fine. I got some money in return. After that the excuses started. "We can't do this … you've got to understand it's tied up here …" A whole bunch of excuses! Okay, I believed my friends. They sounded sincere, so I believed them. I let it go and forgot about it for a little while.

Then there came a time when I wanted to go to Vancouver. My daughter had just given birth to my first grandchild and I wanted to go visit them. I also missed my son, who was there also. I decided to write to the friends who were handling the money. They did give me some holdings, but they wanted them back, and I very nicely signed them over. The bank told me not to do it, but I explained, "Oh, I trust this man. He's not going to do anything wrong with it. He needs it now." So I gave it to him.

This was a grave error on my part. I was stupid, of course. I don't even want to mention the amount of money I handed over to these people because it kills me just the thought of how bad it was. I lost it all. Maybe I had to be stripped of everything before I could start to see who I really was. All the years I had been married to Hymie, he kept me in a dollhouse. I hid my life behind his. He used to tell our children, "Let's not worry your mother. She lives on Cloud Nine. Let's leave her there." So I really didn't know what working on this planet was all about. I didn't realize that other people were not as sincere as I thought they were, that they could be so quick to lie and cheat others.

After Hymie's death there were instances when he revealed himself to me in spirit. Once while I was having an exhibition of my paintings, I had to carry a heavy stack of paintings from one hall into another, and there was no one around to help me. Unexpectedly, I lost my balance and felt I was going to drop the load I was carrying. Then, suddenly, I felt the burden lifted from my arms. Incredibly, I was able to carry all those paintings on just one finger. I knew then that Hymie was there, helping me carry them all.

Another time was during a snowstorm, when I was driving by myself and the car spun and skidded off the road into a snow bank. There was no other traffic around and I began to panic. I could not get the car to budge, and I was in tears. All of a sudden, something lifted the car up into the air and literally turned it around. Hymie had again come to my rescue.

I moved to Vancouver to be closer to my daughter and granddaughter, and left my son in Montreal. The year was 1971, in the spring, and three years had passed since Hymie's death. I had a strong pull toward my granddaughter. Every time I heard a baby cry, I felt she needed me. To this day my granddaughter and I are very close. There seems to be something there, some bond between us—I'm not sure what it is.

One time I agreed to go out with a man, a friend of mine who was substituting as a teacher at the university. He was a mathematician. I'll call him Mike. As we drove down Fourth Avenue, I looked out the window and saw this second-hand store. There was a lot of junk lying around outside the shop. It didn't look like the kind of store you would want to go into. It didn't even look clean, for that matter. I said to Mike, "Stop the car. I'd like to go into that shop."

Well, Mike chuckled and said, "*That* shop? Look at it. You want to go inside *there*?"

I told him again to stop the car. "If you won't take me in, I'll go by myself."

"Well, all right," he grumbled. After all, I was his date. He stopped and we parked the car, then went in.

I really didn't notice the man inside the shop right away. He sort of blended in with the interior. He was a man who looked to be in his mid or late forties. He had long black hair and a sort of sallow or light brown complexion. He wore light brown, baggy pants and a shirt. I didn't notice his eyes then because he wasn't looking at me. I walked around and said to myself, "What am I doing here?"

Meanwhile, Mike, being a mathematician, walked over to this man and saw him doing some equations. Mike said, "Oh ... my ... what is it you're doing there? What are all these equations?"

The man turned to him and said, "It's not of this world."

I overheard the remark and slapped my cheek as I said to myself, "Dear God, a nut!"

Well, just at that moment the man turned and looked at me. He had huge, saucer-shaped eyes that looked black from where I stood. He looked right at me and he smiled. I thought to myself, he has read my mind!

Mike tried to get some answers out of him, but was having no luck. I looked around the store, trying to find something to buy ... anything. I finally settled on some doo-dad and brought it up to the counter. In a cocky fashion I asked the man, "Well, when are they going to take me?" I was, of course, referring to the experience I had had in college, when the two people in wet suit gear had appeared at my bedside.

The man kept a straight face as he told me, "I'll find out."

**The Second Hand Store
on Fourth Avenue in Vancouver
1971 to 1973**

That answer intrigued me, and I thought, my God, what does he mean?

As Mike and I walked out of the shop, Mike said, "Good God, whatever he was doing in there … that math made my knowledge look primitive! What's going on here? I feel like I don't know anything now."

Little did I know that for years my mathematician friend went searching for this man. He always went to another street, however. He thought it was Broadway. I was told later by my contact that they purposely confused him by making him believe the shop was on Broadway instead of Fourth Avenue. They had no interest in Mike. It was me they wanted. This was their way of getting the message to me. Another friend of mine told me not to bother going out with the mathematician again. Without my even knowing him, the friend already stipulated that I should not be seeing this mathematician, that he was very negative and would not be good for me. So I took his advice.

I kept going back to the shop to see the man named Frank. I was drawn. I just had to go back. Three or four times a week I would go to the shop, and he was always there. Frank was not the owner, but he worked there. Once I talked to the owner of the shop and he told me that Frank had simply shown up one day. "How do you like this man?" the shop owner said to me. "Frank came in one day and he right away made himself available here. In electronics he's a genius!"

Frank told me various things that eventually convinced me he was an alien. At first I thought maybe he was just reading all of this from somewhere. There were plenty of books on the subject, after all. But when he started showing me things with the electronics, I knew he was no ordinary man. I saw him tune in to another planet on a television set.

It was all crystal-like. I saw people walking who had floating capes. The capes were all different colors, and they had different shoes as well, sort of turned up, like slippers. The people appeared happy—they smiled a lot. I was fascinated with the capes because the capes seemed to move with the people. It was a different kind of material from anything I've seen.

Some of the homes on other planets are absolutely gorgeous. I was shown the inside of one of the houses. Their homes are somewhat like silos—round in shape. For instance, there were sunken living rooms, circular parts where one is an eating area and the other is a music and a reading room.

I saw cities made of crystal with lots of underground passages.

Everything appeared circular. Their homes were made of crystals, but in circular domes. It was just gorgeous!

He probably let me view this beautiful scene for close to five minutes. He zoomed in on some close features of some of the people that were there, and they had high eyebrows. Their eyes were very slick, almost like Oriental people or the Egyptians with the big lines. It seemed to be natural, not any sort of makeup they were wearing. Their eyes could reveal so much. I could see that they were simply happy.

Frank could make scenes appear on the screen. I thought at first, well, maybe he can do that with a picture. I was looking for excuses, you see. He spoke in a foreign language. He would show me aliens from his craft.

When I would come to the shop, usually nobody would be there, so Frank and I had time. After six months I accepted him, and once he knew I had accepted him, he began to tell me things. He told me that I had to be in contact with him, that he was responsible for four people and I was one of them.

Sometimes I would walk into the shop when no one else was there and, being psychic, I could feel another presence. I would say to Frank, "Okay, who else is in this room?" He would smile and say, "You're right. They came in here to see you." I could actually feel them. If he had said that and I didn't feel them, I wouldn't buy it. I felt them. I knew them.

Frank knew everything about me, it seemed. He knew when I had lost my first husband, how I felt about my life in general, and how I felt I was an alien to this planet. He even mentioned to me that since I had searched and since I had dealt with as much as I had, it was the right time for me to be here.

As the expression goes, when you are ready, the master appears—and here he was. Frank told me things that nobody would ever know about my personal life. He showed me a clock where my first husband was. Hymie was at Number 12, and I was at Number 7. I had to get to 6 and 5 and 4, or the other way around, to get to be a 12. Frank told me Hymie was mapping out my life and helping me, and because his love was still there and he has also reached the very highest plateau, they were in contact with him.

Frank talked about my paintings as having a spiritual quality that very few people could understand or grasp the meaning. I once brought in crayon sketches for Frank, which he liked very much. Then when I saw him a few days later, he had transformed the sketches into something that resembled thin, beaten, copper-plated things by a process with which we have no understanding. He told me this art work was then passed on to a higher authority.

He said that eventually I would change my way of painting, and that they were giving me a new way of painting. There were messages in my work. As a matter of fact, a gentleman friend of mine can read my paintings. It has to do with the spiritual evolution of man and the messages that are in there. Frank also said that because my paintings were of a New Age, I wouldn't be accepted on this planet because they are paintings of the future, and Earth is not ready for me. But everything that I was painting would be transmitted elsewhere because they required what I was doing. I have an insight or a sort of 'psychic opening' where they can at least contact me and give me an idea. All I ask for is an idea. For example, with one of my paintings, called *Motion*, all I got was the word *motion* and from that I just went ahead.

Another time he showed me some moon dust on his work bench, with a pale blue light that glowed once all the room lights were extinguished. Frank claimed he could astral travel to the moon. He once showed me on his television the image of an abandoned UFO into the mountains near Harrison Hot Springs in British Columbia, in a wooded area. There was no transmission whatsoever on the television set—in other words, when nothing was on—Frank could project pictures. I don't know how he did that.

Spirituality is very important. Frank and I talked a lot about spirituality. He told me that on his planet people are highly evolved and everybody loves each other. Even though there are various people who look different, they are accepted without any racial prejudice. Their way of life is what I would hope someday to see on Earth. You would be able to go to bed without locking your door, and nobody would care that you had more than they had. Being evolved, you could accept all this without feeling any pangs of anxiety.

Everything manufactured on Frank's planet lasted. Here on Earth things are made but they don't last. Things break and you have to go out and buy a replacement. That's the way our economy works. Their economy is totally different.

Oftentimes Frank picked up auras of people who walked into the shop. Sometimes they were good vibrations and sometimes not—even to the point of being terrible. For example, a couple of nice people walked into the shop one day and he said to me, "My God ... terrible ... terrible vibration."

I said to Frank, "How can you say that?" I was reprimanding him. I asked, "How can you know that?" He would never answer. He would just smile. To me, that was truth.

Once when I asked him why he was here, Frank said to me, "I'm here because you love God so much."

Testing him, I said, "Okay, which God is that?"

He said, "There's only one Creator. We all belong to the Creator." That was a good enough answer for me.

Chapter 3

Arne and the Karmic Months

I met Arne on his birthday, November 10, 1971. When Arne Moller first met me, he said to himself and later to me, "I have to do something for you. I don't know what it is, but I know you from somewhere." Just like that. I didn't pick up on him, however.

Arne was tall, good-looking, soft-spoken and gentle—one of those tall Danish guys. I started going out with him, and then one day I walked in to see Frank and I said to Frank, "I'm going to bring you a guy I want you to meet."

He said, "Sure, bring him in." Frank *knew.*

Well, as soon as I brought Arne into the shop to meet Frank, Arne accepted him immediately. It had taken me six months, but Arne accepted Frank right away—which I thought was really strange. Arne began asking him questions. He had a lot of questions, and he got his answers.

There was a reason why Arne came into my life. Frank would not tell me about my own karma. But that's how Arne and I came into being. Arne had been a Roman soldier. He had arrested me in a past life. Things were bad between us—so bad, in fact, that we had to neutralize the karma through a marriage. My contact also told Arne that I would be with him only a short time.

Shortly after Frank met Arne, Arne asked me to marry him and I asked Frank's advice. Frank didn't even look at me. He said, "Marry him immediately."

A little shocked, I replied, "But I don't know if I even love this man!" I liked Arne. In many ways he reminded me a little bit of Hymie. I was always searching for another Hymie, which was my problem. Well, I decided I'd listen to Frank, so I said, "Okay, will you come to the wedding?"

He said, "I can't. There's one other person there that has such a high vibration. I can't be in contact with that person." I still don't understand to this day what he was talking about. Was it possible the two of them would clash? Or would they know each other and it wouldn't be to my advantage? I just don't know why. That has always puzzled me.

Before I married Arne, my sister Mary had a visitation from Hymie, in which all the paintings that I had made and given to her fell off the wall. This is one thing I have never been able to understand. I do not know if Hymie didn't want me to marry Arne or what. What I feel happened is that perhaps other powers wanted to put a stop to the marriage, and they conjured up an image of Hymie so that my mother became frightened as well.

So Arne and I got married, against my mother's wishes. Arne was not Jewish, so my mother even went so far as to send my brother-in-law Leonard to stop the wedding. She paid for his ticket to come out to Vancouver and convince me not to marry Arne. But it didn't work.

I now feel this was an important test. I could have very nicely backed out of the marriage to Arne, but I didn't. The reason I didn't was because I believed in Frank. Once I tested Frank to my own gratification, I knew that he was an authentic alien. Spiritually all the qualities were there that I required. When I told myself, "Yes, Frank is an alien, he is of the spiritual matter I am interested in," then I went along with Frank all the way.

When I married Arne, he was in stocks and bonds and tangible things. Within one month he lost his job. From that point on things went from bad to worse, because if there is no money, everything flies out the window.

In those days I kept running to my contact constantly. Frank never said anything. I yelled. I screamed. I said, "How could you do this to me?" I was really like a child crying, "Look at what you did!" Frank never said a word.

I went to work in order to help make ends meet. Things were very bad between Arne and me. I yelled and screamed at Frank, and Frank said to me, "Why don't you tell Arne to go to such-and-such a place and he'll get a job."

So, following Frank's advice, we drove out to the country. We were living in my small apartment in Vancouver at that time, and we went out to Surrey, to a farm that needed a farm hand. Arne, who had lived amongst cattle in Denmark and knew all about farm life, decided he would take the job.

The farmers gave us a house to live in, so we didn't have to pay rent. We didn't have to pay for electricity, although we did pay for our telephone. They paid Arne one hundred dollars a month wage, but it still was not enough. I still had to work, so I went to Vancouver, which was thirty miles away. I had to commute sixty miles two or three days a week. Being an artist, I still had to have time for my work. I felt like I was fighting for my dear life and there was just never enough time for myself.

I would drop in and see Frank. He was with me through all of that period, and we did our best. When I would come in and complain to Frank that I couldn't take this kind of life any longer, he would start to say, "But you have to be there ..." and then he would cut himself off. He was trying to tell me that I had to spend X amount of years in such an environment, and that was that. So if I didn't do it now, I would have to make up for it later. But at the time I was unaware of this. He stopped himself in time so as not to interfere.

Another example of Frank almost letting the cat out of the bag was on my birthday. Arne and I would sort of meditate a couple of times a week, and one day, on my birthday, I was sitting and reading. Suddenly I had flashes in my mind. I felt a lot of buzzing, which meant a lot of the aliens were in. I saw spacecraft—all different kinds of spacecraft—they were gorgeous! So I drove into town and I said to Frank, "Look at what I saw! All these spacecraft!"

Frank said, "Yes, we wanted you to see them. We wanted

to let you know the different types of spacecraft that there are."

I said, "I'm moving into town."

In protest, Frank told me, "But you're supposed to stay ... " and he cut himself off again.

We moved into town. Since I was working, I told Arne to go and find a place for us. He found a place we could move into, so we went ahead. We had the movers. My son, Ron, was helping, as well as Arne. We had everything in the vestibule of the new place when the owner came out and told us, "We have decided we don't want you here." Then, because the door was locked, we had to wait for the manager before we could retrieve all our things.

Disgusted, we put everything back into the rented van. Then we went looking for a house, an apartment, anything. Finally, at 11:00 that night, we got into a place.

The next day I trooped down to see Frank. "Look what's happened!" I yelled. Frank said not a word. *Not one word!*

Arne made up his mind he couldn't get a job in Vancouver. He thought he could get a job in Australia. So we decided to sell some of our things. This was very hard for me. Little did I know at the time that Frank had talked to Arne. He had said, "If she doesn't start to detach herself from her material belongings, I'm washing my hands of her, because this is her last lifetime. She's been sitting on the fence long enough. Either she does something about it or ... " Arne didn't tell me then because he was promised to secrecy. I found that out on my own. But every time I sold something, it tore something from me. It hurt me every time I sold something because I would remember that Hymie and I had saved money to buy a particular piece of crystal. I saw everything going and I hated it.

Then one day I went into the shop and Frank looked at me and said, "Don't sell everything. You'll need some of it." He was pleased that I was slowly letting go of things. At first I was terribly hurt, but eventually it subsided. Then I felt better. I learned that lesson. After that I didn't care anymore. It was no longer important. But I didn't know that then. Arne told me all of this much later on. When Frank said to me, "Don't sell everything, you'll need something for yourself," whatever it was that felt right, I kept.

Frank kept in contact with me for two years, from 1971 to 1973, in order to raise my consciousness and to help me get rid of a lot of my karmic debts. He helped me to detach myself from my material aspects. When I got enough money to send Arne down to Australia, Frank said, "Good, that's where he's supposed to go."

When I sent Arne down to Australia, my new life began. The teachings started for me. Frank said, "Since you've had such a hard life and could not find a place for yourself, we want to help you. People have hurt you a great deal, your sensitivity is at such a low point ... we are going to protect you. Anybody who ever hurts you in any way will suffer the consequences." Frank then told me there are seven people looking after this planet, and he had spoken to them because he wanted to take on my karmic conditions and all the various experiences for me. They told him no. That I would have to go through everything myself because that's the only way I'm going to learn.

I said to my contact, "You're willing to do this because you care for me that much?"

Frank looked at me and he said, "Yes, I do."

I was quite overwhelmed.

Before Arne went down to Australia, Frank had given him a special belt to take wherever he went, and in that way Frank would electronically have a beeping light so that he knew where Arne was at all times. Then Frank could go visit him to see how he was doing. Frank would not tell me how Arne was doing.

Meanwhile, I didn't hear from Arne. I wrote to him, asked him how he was doing, and I learned that he had gotten a job. Arne wanted to send me money so that I could have enough to join him in Australia. He never did send me any money. I wasn't happy about our relationship. I knew within myself that I had to rectify everything because of my mistake. I knew that the time would come when I would leave Arne, but it had to be when he was in a good position, and not when he was down and out. I couldn't do that. Little did I know that this was one of the tests.

I kept asking Frank, "Do you think I should go down to Australia now?" No answer. He never gave me a yes or a no as to what I should do. I had to decide that myself. All this time while Arne was in Australia, waiting for me to come down, Frank kept track of him with the beeping red light. He knew exactly where Arne was, and so forth. Finally a letter came from Arne and I said to Frank, "I think I have to go down." So I sold the rest of my things.

A funny thing happened as we shipped a lot of our stuff down to Australia. I asked Frank, "What am I going to do with my art? I'm taking my art."

He said, "If you take your art, I will sink the boat."

"No, no, no! Don't do that!" I protested.

"We have discussed it," he told me. "You're allowed to take two paintings with you."

"Just two?" I was dumbfounded. I said, "I want four."

He said, "Two."

"I want *four!*"

"Okay," he finally agreed. He let me take four. I shouldn't have taken any. Then I asked him, "Where am I going to put all the art pieces?"

He said, "They're very important. All your work is very important."

The next day I got a call from a friend of mine. "Tell me, what are you going to do with all your paintings?"

I said I didn't know what to do.

She said, "Look, why don't you use my basement? I don't know for how long. Maybe for a year or so, but how about it?"

So I called up Frank and he said fine. It's just like he *knew.* He said, "I'll send a truck around and pick up everything, and we'll bring it there." He took care of everything.

The time drew nearer for me to leave for Australia. Frank gave me a disc, like one he had also given Arne. I didn't know what the meaning of the disc was, but I accepted it without questioning him. Sometimes I think if I knew as much then as I know today, I would have asked many more questions. I once asked, "Where are you from, Frank?" He told me very far away. "Where very far away?" Why didn't I insist on him answering that? Why didn't I take a photograph of him?

I once had a two-page letter Frank had written which contained his alien writing. I sent that letter to a group called CSI, which claimed to have contact with aliens. When Frank found out, he was furious. I suppose the person who received the letter freaked out because it was so obvious that the writing was not of this Earth. Now I wish I had a copy of that letter. Why hadn't I photocopied it? Why didn't I do a lot of things? Why I didn't do these things, I have no idea. But I may have been stopped. I may have been stopped from doing a lot of things.

I gave up my apartment and stayed at my daughter's home. I was there maybe two months, and then decided around Christmastime to go to Australia. I said to Frank, "I think now I'm ready to go down."

He said, "Fine." He handed me a belt, a very special belt that he put various things inside. I met a healer who examined the belt and he said right away, "Oh, this is powerful! Don't leave home without it." I now wear this belt whenever I travel.

Frank told me, "If ever you have to go on a trip and there's no spacecraft available to look after you, a fog will come and you will not go." I travel a lot, and every time I see a fog coming, my trip is cancelled. So whenever I travel, I smile because I know there's always a spacecraft coming with me.

For instance, recently my present husband Fred and I went to Reno, and I looked out the cabin window of the jet and there was a spacecraft. I showed it to Fred and said, "Take a look at those three colors. Yellow, red, green ... "

"Oh, that's a beacon," he replied.

I said, "How can it be a beacon way up in the sky?"

When we returned from Reno, a friend of mine asked, "Didn't you see a spacecraft going to Reno? I know you always have one."

I said, "Yes."

Fred said, "She said that was a spacecraft."

And I said, "What did you say? It was a beacon?"

So this guy laughed, too.

Anyway, I now had my ticket and everything, I was ready to join Arne in Australia. Before I left, I had to say goodbye to my son, Ronny. He was very disturbed that I was leaving. I gave him my car and various things and told him, "Why don't you go back to Montreal?" Then I told him if he needed money to sell the car. Saying goodbye to my daughter, Sharon, wasn't that upsetting, but with my son it really bothered me. Ron's whole life seemed to change afterwards when he went to Montreal and married a woman that he wasn't happy with. I think he was pretty attached to me. He had no father, and with my going to Australia, he didn't know when he would see me again. He thought I was going there permanently. There must have been quite a feeling of abandonment on his part.

Frank had given me the belt and he said to me, "I'll come every now and then and see you."

I felt comforted at his words, and without knowing what lay ahead of me, headed for the airport.

Chapter 4

With Flying Colors

The Vancouver airport was crowded. As I stood in line to check my baggage, the girl behind the counter said, "I'm sorry, ma'am, but you have too much weight."

Sudden panic seized me. I turned around and faced the man standing in line behind me. He had hardly any luggage at all. "You have very little luggage," I said. "Would you mind taking some of my poundage on yours?"

He shrugged good-naturedly and said, "Gladly."

So that's how I got through with my typewriter and all the various things I took with me to Australia. At the time I thought I was going there for good. I didn't realize it would be only for six months. Arne knew it, but I did not.

When I arrived in Australia, I waited a long time for Arne to meet me at the airport. I had sent him a cable, telling him I was coming. I waited and waited, but there was no sign of him. There I stood with all my luggage in a foreign country with nobody to meet me.

Finally, the man from customs came over to me and asked, "Who are you waiting for?"

"My husband."

"That bloke? Don't worry about it. If that bloke doesn't come along, there will be another bloke."

Well, that certainly didn't make me feel any better. I couldn't figure out what had happened to Arne, why he wasn't there to meet me.

Finally, unable to wait any longer, I called a cab and directed the driver to take me to Arne's last known address. I had no choice but to go to meet him. When I arrived there, I rang the bell. I guessed Arne might be working.

A man came to the door and I asked, "Does Arne Moller live here?"

"Nope. Nobody by that name lives here," he said.

"But that's impossible!" I waved the piece of paper with Arne's address in front of his face. "This is his last address."

"Nobody by that name lives here."

Puzzled and a trifle upset, I said, "Okay, give me the name and address of whoever owns this apartment."

He gave me the information I wanted and I got back into the cab. Then we went to find the apartment building's owner.

"Look," the building's owner told me, "I don't know. It's possible he doesn't live there." Then he looked at me and stroked his chin. "Maybe he doesn't want to be found."

By this time I was feeling outraged. "Listen, that's not true!"

The apartment owner shrugged and started to close his door. "Sorry … I can't do anything … "

I stepped forward to keep the door from shutting in my face. "Now you wait a minute," I said to him. "If I don't hear from you shortly, I'm going to the police!"

"Okay! Okay! Don't do that," he said. "I have a manager who takes care of that building. Maybe he can find something out for you. Let me get hold of him, and then he will contact you. Where will you be staying?"

I looked at the taxi driver and asked, "Which is the closest hotel?"

The driver gave me a name, so I told this to the man, then said, "Okay, if I don't hear by a certain time, I'm going to the authorities whether you like it or not."

The cab driver took me to the nearest hotel. I watched the exchange with a sinking feeling. It was to our dollar one dollar and forty-four there, so I lost money right away. I thought to myself, "My God, I don't have enough money!" I had only purchased a one-way ticket. What if I didn't find Arne? How was I ever going to get back? What was I going to do?

At this point I began to panic. Up in my room, I said, "Frank!" I was really upset. "Frank, what is this all about?" Then I calmed down. I told myself, "Well, you know all this. There must be a reason for all this. Okay, what is the reason?"

Then the telephone rang. It was the manager of the apartment building. "Yes, ma'am, there is a man by the name of Arne Moller who does live there," he told me.

Thank God! At least I got the right person.

The manager told me Arne came home from work at five o'clock, so I said fine, hung up, and called another cab and went to wait for Arne.

As soon as Arne saw me I knew he wasn't expecting me. "Didn't you get my cable?"

"No," he said. "I got nothing."

"Fantastic," I grumbled. I discovered he was living in a very small place, not even large enough for two people. He was working at a menial job, not making much money. He managed to get me into another place temporarily and this was how we commuted for a while until I said, "Arne, this just isn't going to work. For all I've gone through ... I sold all my things ... for what? For this menial job you've found? My God, what is this?"

What it was, of course, was that I was being tested. I was being shown that I had the ability to do something about things, where before I had always submerged myself into my first husband. Hymie had looked after everything then. I thought I didn't know how to handle things. It wasn't true. I *could* handle everything. There was a purpose in all this ... to prove to myself that I *could* handle every situation.

Meanwhile the merchandise which I had sent down to Australia from Canada didn't come. It went to Melbourne instead. In fact, it seemed to go everywhere else except where it was supposed to go! What I didn't know was that they were holding it back, since we didn't have an apartment yet.

Nothing right was going for us. So I decided to take matters into my own hands. I called up the Jewish community center, where there was a support group. We attended a dance sponsored by this community center, where I thought I could meet some people. I didn't realize it was a singles dance. All the men came running up to me, and I thought, "My God, what is this?" Then once I realized what it was, I said, "That's my husband over there, you know."

One of the men asked me, "What are you doing here?"

"I'm looking for a place," I replied. You had to have six months rent before you could get into a place, and I didn't have that kind of money. I only had a little bit of money left, and that was all there was. I didn't have anything else.

The man looked at me and said, "I have an apartment empty. You take it."

"Just like that?" I asked.

He said, "You're a Jewish girl. I won't ask anything from you. Just pay the rent every month."

I said, "Fine." That day Arne got a call and found out that all our stuff was coming from Melbourne. We arranged to move into this place.

One day shortly after that, I walked into a gallery because we needed some money. Arne's menial job was just not enough. I went up to the art director with one of my small paintings that I had. Right away he said, "Oh, we're not interested. We have enough artists. We especially don't need out-of-town artists."

I didn't know what to do then. It's strange how things work out, however. I was going to start wrapping up my painting when a woman walked in, a customer, and she spotted my work. "Oh! That's the painting I want!" she exclaimed.

The art director winked at me to shut me up, and I got the message. I said to her, "Oh, do you really like it?"

She said, "I love it! Of all the paintings, that's what I want."

I said to the director, "Fine, you make the price." So he gave the price, and when it was all settled, the woman picked out a frame and then she walked out.

The art director turned to me and said, "Look, I know we don't do this, but ... could you bring me some other paintings that you've got?"

"Well, I don't have very much right now," I told him. "I have to start making more. I just happened to paint this one, and I just thought I'd see what you said about it."

Talk about being saved by the bell—I tell you! And then I told him I didn't have a telephone, that if he wanted to contact me he could send a telegram—which he did. He asked me to come to work for him, to do P.R. work and paint, if I wanted, on weekends. He would pay me so much, and then I would learn all about the Australian artists.

I was so happy. Then I received word that a gallery in Vancouver, where I had left some paintings, had just sold a piece of art, so I got that money. This was how they helped me.

I worked on Arne to such a degree that he got inspired. He went out and found himself a really good job. He became a diesel engineer for the Sydney government, and this made him happy.

Then I went out and got myself another job, selling shoes. In order to retain my job I had to sell fifty pairs of shoes. The selling itself was not too bad. Finding where the stock was and everything nearly drove me mad. In addition, I was in competition with all the people who worked there. Everybody was younger than I was, yet I managed to keep up. The fact that I was older than everybody else didn't seem to matter. I still had time to sell fifty pairs of shoes and give my personal touch to the customer.

That came to the ears of my boss, and he called me in one day and said to me, "I'm promoting you into a higher class merchandise." It was a store right next to the shoe store, which sold nothing for less than $150. It was an Italian imports, shoes and bags. I agreed, but he said I needed some training and that he was willing to train me.

I started the first day and got higher wages, which made me feel really good. Then I said to myself, "Okay, is this a test?" You see, I was beginning to be, as my contact said, pretty clever in noticing when the tests came around. For one thing, I was saving money to go back to Canada. I wasn't going to stay in

Australia. This wasn't my permanent residence. Once Arne got his better job that I had inspired him to get and he was doing well, my plan was to tell him, "Arne, I'm leaving."

There were other tests that I noticed. In Australia, they threw various men at me. One, in particular, was very significant because he reminded me of one of my pasts, and I was very much taken by this person, whom I'll call Richard. I think Richard was one of my husbands many eons ago. Anyway, Richard was married, but we used to meet at lunchtime only and talk about books. We read the same books and we had a lot to communicate with each other. Little did I know at the time that he was falling for me. I liked him, but I would never do anything to jeopardize anybody's life. To me, that's definitely taboo.

One day Richard said to me, "You're leaving, aren't you?" I said, "Yes."

He said, "Well, why don't I take you out this evening? No harm in that."

I said, "No, I guess not." He talked me into going out to dinner with him. And as it turned out, Richard did make advances toward me, but I put a stop to that. I told him, "If that's the case, take me home."

Richard was immediately apologetic and said, "Okay, I won't."

I told him I liked him very much just to talk to, and that I wanted him to tell his wife we were dining together. "I wish you'd have brought her along." But you see, it was a test. They wanted to find out if I would encroach on somebody else's territory, and if I would lie to Arne.

When I told Arne Richard had invited me out, Arne went, "Ah-ha! So that's what's going on."

I said to Arne, "Don't you trust me? I will never cheat on anybody. Infidelity — I will not! I don't buy that. Everything is up and up with me in every way."

Another test occurred when there was money left open.

I was there and nobody else was around. In other words, I could have taken that money. I did not. Another time, I was in a supermarket and the cashier handed me back twenty extra dollars. I very nicely handed it back to her. I did not realize at the time that these were all tests. I was told afterwards.

They tested me on every aspect of how I would behave. Then I started to know when they were tests, because I became aware of them. There were just too many incidences all at once. Finally I had to say, "Okay, guys, you're doing terrific." Then the testing stopped. They didn't have to test me anymore because I already knew they were tests, and they knew what my nature was. That's all they were interested in—to see if I could carry on the role they wanted to give me.

Now here I was, working at the shoe store, doing P.R. work on the side, and all this to save enough money so I could leave. Yet my boss was going to spend money on me to train me. I wondered what I should do. Should I not tell him anything and take the job, which was enticing to me? Or should I tell him the truth?

These were the questions I wrestled with. After two weeks, I went into the job and I really liked it. I truly liked it. Because so many things were happening to me, I said, "Okay, upstairs, dish it up. I don't care. I want to get through with my karma."

As soon as I said that, as soon as I made up my mind that I was going to do everything anyway, no matter how hard, it came easier. That's how this new job had come into being. So I had a lot to wrestle with. "Do you want me to take this job and continue in it, and make money and lie about the fact that I'm not going to be permanent here? What am I going to do?"

I decided to tell my boss. I walked into the manager and I told him that I was saving my money to return to Canada, that this wasn't going to be my permanent home. I then told him that I appreciated all he was doing for me, and that I would like to get back my old job.

Well, first of all, he sat—stunned. Then he said, "I have

never in my life met somebody like you. Here you have a raise in wages. You have a posh job ... all the wonderful things ... and you're telling me not to spend money on you because you are leaving? I can't believe it!" Then he added, "But you did give me back my faith in humanity."

I said, "Thank you. Now can I get my old job back?"

He said no.

"How come ... if I've done this for you?"

"Well," he said, "because I know you're leaving. What good is that?"

So I lost my job altogether. All I had left was the gallery job.

On Friday, April 6, 1973, just the day before I broke my news to the store manager, I had had a dream at 3 a.m. In the dream I saw a wisp of white smoke near a doorway, watched it and saw something flying toward me. It was a small airplane. It had deep navy green colors. It got hold of my finger and pulled it. It chewed my finger, and I moaned, and Arne woke me up. That dream was to tell me it was time to go and get an airline ticket and fly back to Canada. I didn't tell Arne about the dream. I went and bought my airline ticket.

Then I finally told Arne, and he practically started to cry. "I know Frank told me you'd only be with me six months," he revealed.

I said, "Why didn't you tell me?"

"Because I promised not to tell."

When we visited with our group of friends, one of the men told Arne, "Since you are an Australian, Arne, you could stop your wife from leaving the country." In Australia at that time it was legal for men to put claims on their wives. Women's rights were not the same as in North America. A man's wife was his property.

But Arne told his friend, "Listen, I wouldn't start up with her at all, because my life would be endlessly in jeopardy. I would have hell to pay for it! No ... she wants to go, it's her time to go."

I told Arne he was being watched by the beeping light. Then I took pictures of certain sections where my contact showed me where the spacecraft were, wherever I was—all around. Now because Arne became negative, they dropped Arne—just like that. He fulfilled his mission with me. I would never have gone down to Australia without him. Since he had been a Roman soldier in a past life, he had to make up for that—we both did— by neutralizing our relationship through a marriage, which we did. All together we were married one year. He wrote to me for a solid year after that, and then we drifted apart. I had new paths to follow.

Chapter 5

Mission of Importance

Picking up the telephone, I dialed the familiar number, then listened to the ringing on the other end. When he answered, I said, "Frank, I'm back!"

Right away he said, "What took you so long?"

I hadn't told Frank I was coming back, but I wasn't surprised that he knew. "Frank, I think I did fantastic."

He said, "We're all proud of you."

"I'm coming down to see you," I said and hung up.

When I got to the shop, Frank took the bracelet that he had given me before I had gone to Australia and he rubbed it. There was a lot of Frank's writing on the bracelet, consisting of hieroglyphics type symbols, and he rubbed all over that. Then he looked at the bracelet, and then at me, and he said, "You're an eight."

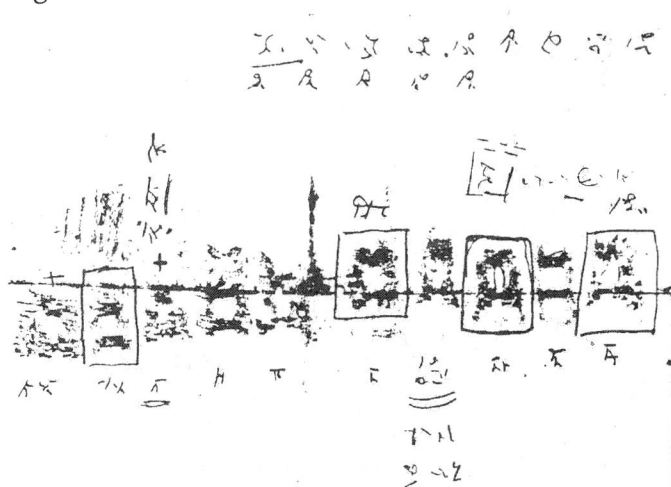

The bracelet rubbing

"I'm a what?"

"You're an eight." He smiled. He seemed very impressed by the fact that I was an eight, but I had no idea what that meant.

"Well, I hope that's good," I said. I didn't ask him what being an eight meant because I thought it had to be quite good being an eight. He was certainly impressed, at least. Apparently all the tests I had gone through had placed me on the eighth rung of the spiritual ladder—whatever that means.

Frank then asked me for the disc he had given me. He removed some items from it and colored it in. Then he broke off various things which showed where I was at. Pictured on the disc is the likeness of a queen or the high priestess which is found on tarot cards. Not only one psychic, but at least three who have held this disc in their hands have had this message come through that has to do with a tarot card of the priestess.

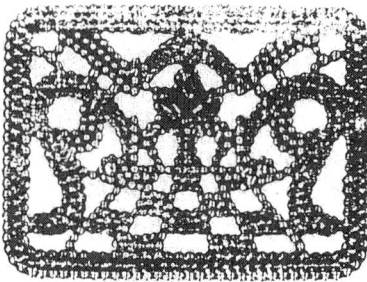

The disk showing the High Priestess

Arne's

Shirlé's

When I came back again to see Frank at the shop, he began to tell me what plans were in store for me. "We have tested you," he said, "and you have passed every test. We're very proud of you. We now want you to gather the people."

"What people?" I asked. "What are you talking about?"

"We want you to gather the people," Frank repeated.

"What ... Frank, please don't do this to me. What am I? I don't know enough. I'm not intellectual enough. All I've got is one stupid little degree. I'm nothing."

"Shirlè ... "

"What about the government people?" I raved. "What about the scientists?"

"We don't want them," he said. "They're too much on an ego trip."

"But I ... "

"Don't say anymore. We've chosen you, and that's that."

Chosen me? Chosen me for what, I wondered. I said, "Okay, do you think I'm capable? I mean, Frank ... really, I'm just ... "

"I don't want to hear another word, Shirlè. This is it!"

I saw how serious he was then. "Okay," I said, "what am I supposed to do?"

"You're going to gather the people."

"*What* people?" I demanded. "Who? What? When? Frank, I don't follow you!"

He looked at some sort of disc and then he turned to me. "People of your vibration," he said.

"What do you mean by that?" I asked.

He looked at me patiently. "You know very well what I mean. There will be people that have your vibration. You're very high on the spiritual level. You have all the abilities and the love that is required. Don't worry about it. There will come a time ... " I must have looked startled. Frank smiled to reassure me. "Now, nothing is a certainly, but we have to prepare for it, just in case the time comes when it is uninhabitable here.

We're going to save a segment of the population ... "

"Oh, what do you mean a *segment* of the population?" I cried. "You mean, you're not going to save *everybody*?"

He shook his head. "No, we're not."

"But you have to save everybody!" I was quite worked up by now. "How can you say you're not going to save everybody? You *have* to!"

After I finished my ranting and raving, Frank said to me in a calm voice, "Are you finished?" Then he went on, "We're saving a segment of the population, and you'll understand later on."

I sat back and folded my hands in my lap.

"These are the people that we're going to help," Frank continued. "Now, I'll show you where the landing is going to be. The landing is going to be between the United States and Canada. It's in Surrey." He told me the exact point, but I am not going to mention where exactly. All I will say is that there is a marker point there. The farm Arne and I had lived on near Surrey was on the border between the United States and Canada. On that border Frank put various devices. He said that was where the landing was going to be.

He told me that when the farmer wanted to sell his house it would not sell for a long, long time. It has sold since then, which is close to eight years after he told me this, but that land is still there and the cows graze like before. Arne and I once walked out onto the field, looking for some device, and when we went around various poles, there was a certain eerie feeling. Arne, being very psychic as well, could pick up that some high frequency was around. When the ley-lines cross, there are a lot of UFO sightings in that area.

Frank said, "There will be a spacecraft. When the time is right, you're going to bring everybody to the spacecraft."

"Okay," I said, "why are you telling me all this? It's not going to be in my lifetime. After all, I'm not getting any younger!"

"It *is* in your lifetime," he said. "As I said before, we have chosen you. You are going to lead the people. We are going to take a lot of the children. A lot of the children will be taken away from their parents because their parents are not going to make it in this lifetime. You'll be looking after these children. You will have enough help. It will all be worked out. Don't worry. Leave that all up to us. That's not your concern or worry." Then he said, "You are going to be with the people. We have chosen various people. You are one of the teachers."

Again he told me not to worry. "Be watchful, but don't worry, because you are being protected in every shape and form." I wondered how that could be possible, but he explained, "There are beings that are from other places besides the inner levels of realm that can be very destructive ... destructive to humanity ... If anybody ever wants to hurt you ... beware."

This reminds me of an incident once when Frank was talking to me and suddenly he said, "I've got to go. There's a ship coming in and it will be very destructive to humanity." Then he left. Where he went I didn't know. Apparently he called various people to see that they pushed them back—got the harmful spacecraft out before it could hurt anyone.

One day my daughter, Sharon, walked into the shop to meet Frank. She had with her my second grandchild, who was only two months old. Frank said that my grandchildren were both very important to the whole scenario of the future, that they were both very gifted. Now a teenager, my first grandchild is very talented. She writes poetry, sings and hopes to be a journalist. My younger grandchild is a dancer and wants to be a dress designer.

Another time I brought in a friend to meet Frank. I'll call him Bob. I told Frank, "Bob's one of the teachers," and Frank said, "We have enough teachers. We have already chosen ..." And then he shut up. But he gave Bob a silver bracelet. He said Bob was a "silver person." Then, somehow, this person deviated. Bob decided he was going to make his own world. Frank said, "We'll stop him for that." I didn't understand what he meant at the time, but apparently once you reach a high level of spirituality you can project new worlds.

There are some space people who can manufacture a spacecraft from thought. Then they can project through thought and make a new planet. And Bob was determined that he would someday do this. Frank told me, "We will stop him," because Bob, who was more interested in himself, wanted me for a counterpart. "Everybody wants you," said Frank. "We'll put a stop to that." I didn't understand then, but I understand now. Thoughts can create.

Frank also told me that I should go into my paintings, that I should visualize myself and go right into my paintings, "because they are of the higher elements," he said. I am able to see various things there, which is what I try to do. It isn't that easy to do, of course, to go into your paintings.

"Everything that you're going to paint," he told me, "is going to be very important." He then explained that they're giving me secrets from other planets that have been destroyed. Currently I am working on the history of various planets that have been destroyed.

I was also told by Frank that my paintings were of a *healing* nature. "Everybody will come to you for their particular painting," he said. "They will require that." He was referring not only to my *name paintings,* but all of the paintings that I do.

"So now you see why it's important that your paintings have to be watched and looked after," he told me. "After you leave here, you will take all of your paintings with you. They will be compressed into one tiny little suitcase." To draw an analogy, he said, "Just like the Empire State Building could be compressed." That was hard for me to imagine, and I still haven't figured out how that could be.

Frank told me a little about the various planets. On one planet, he said, you use one little card which satisfies all your needs. You do X amount of work of your choice. Schooling is very important because knowledge is very important. They live for a very long time on that planet. They go to school until about the age of 70. They marry once, but they always know exactly whom they will marry, whom to pick, according to their congenial experiences, somehow, and that's how they make their lives. They're not the frivolous kind, apparently. They can be regenerated when they have any illnesses. I was shown so many beautiful things about that particular planet.

There are other planets with underground transportation, in which the dwellings are underground and services are on top of the planet. Everything is clear. There are no tall buildings. It's sort of a compound in a way, and if you want to live in the compound you may, or there are separate dwellings if you prefer. But everything—shopping, transportation, everything—is all above ground. Frank showed me a lot of different places.

He told me about his form. "To contact you," Frank said, "I had to take on a human form. I have borrowed a body." Now, since then, I was told that they can *manufacture* a body. If Frank had told me he could manufacture a body fifteen years ago, I don't know whether I would have understood that, so at the time he said he loaned the body. I have learned since then that he manufactured a body. They can do that. "If you were to see what I really looked like," he told me, "I would scare you."

During a séance in France in 1981, George Major from Sirius-B, came through a medium by the name of Allan McDougall, and said that Frank was from that planet. What was revealed in that séance and others that followed are recorded in a subsequent chapter. Their form is mammalian. They are the ancestors of the dolphins and whales, but they had mutated, actually. They had an atomic war there, and that's why they are petrified of what's going to happen here with all this playing around with negative forces. Atomic explosions are so powerful that they rock other planets out of orbits, which can cause severe problems. Not to mention the waste material that we have, which is absolutely, incredibly awful! Because of it, we are also becoming mutants.

That's why they have to save a certain segment of our population, because we will no longer be what we look like.

They call us a "handsome" race. We're really very beautiful. I don't know if I can say we're much in spirit. I would like to think so, but at least in the physical aspect we are considered handsome. One reason why a lot of the aliens have lost their hair is due to a nuclear holocaust in generations past. They are now in a rather weakened condition. They have degenerated. Some of this was difficult for me to comprehend. Back then I didn't have that much knowledge to go on.

Frank told me to go back to Montreal and try to get back the money I had lost to these friends who had swindled me out of my inheritance after Hymie's passing. Secretly Frank knew I wouldn't see any of the money, but I had to give this man a chance to do the right thing. So I went to Montreal, and this man hemmed and hawed, and said he was going to try, but he didn't.

It wasn't long after this that he was dismissed, so to speak. In other words, he died. I don't know whether they did anything about that, or they knew that he was going to die, but I was to give him this final opportunity to make right the wrong he had caused me. I had to give him a chance to say at least, "Gee, I'll try to do something for you." When I wrote to his wife after his death, she wrote back, "Well, you did loan it to my husband." *She* was my best friend—not her husband! So I let it go.

Frank said to me, "You'll have to go through a few things."

"Oh God, don't tell me *again*," I protested.

He said, "You left Surrey for Vancouver when it wasn't your time. You were supposed to stay a much longer time, but now you're going to have to go through that."

Okay, fine. What else could I say? Then I asked, "What about a man for me in my life? If I have to go through that ... and this time *please* ... make him Jewish ... for my family's sake!"

"Okay," said Frank, "we will do our best."

Then I asked, "How will I know this person?"

"He will say, 'I know you,'" said Frank. "That's how you

will know him. But first there is going to be someone else."
And there *was* someone else—later on.

I had given Frank a book to read, *Sky People*, that I had gotten from Australia and brought back with me. It's written by Brinsley Le Poer Trench and shows from where our history comes, and how we were manufactured. Frank read the book, then told me a few chapters were not true, but everything else in it was authentic. In my opinion it's an excellent book and people will get a tremendous amount of knowledge out of it.

One day while I was on my way to a party, I had a strange experience. Here I was all dressed and ready, driving the car toward my destination, when all of a sudden I felt I simply had to turn the car around and go to the shop to see Frank. The feeling was so strong that I could not ignore it. When I came through the door of the shop, Frank looked at his watch and he said, "Well ... not bad. Fifteen minutes it took you."

I said, "You mean to tell me you *called* me?"

He said, "Yes, we're training you."

Relying on my intuition became important. We all have intuition. It's important to listen to it

Dreams also provide a source of important information for us. One time I went running to Frank with a dream I had had. In the dream I was given a gold disc. I said to Frank, "Gee, I wonder what that meant."

He said, "Well, now you realize you must wear gold."

After I married Fred, my present husband, he also had a dream in which he was given a gold disc. He also must wear gold. Gold rejects the negative.

The time came when Frank called me in. "Listen," he said to me, "I'm getting ready to leave."

I knew it was time to say goodbye.

"Look," he said, "we want you to have something." I don't know how or where it happened, but suddenly in front of my eyes a big sheet appeared, and Frank telepathically received the message which he engraved with a blunt instrument onto this huge metal plate. Then he took another instrument and he cut them up into eighths and he gave them to me.

"What are these?" I asked him.

"We want you to have these," he said. "For the meantime put them in the bank, in a safety deposit box, for safe keeping."

"But … what are they?"

He handed me the eight copper plates, and he said, "They are your driver's license, your medical card, and all the things that you require." In other words, my identification plates.

I accepted that answer at that time. Now I think it's ludicrous that he told me that. It's ridiculous. It just cannot be. But if he had told me how important the plates were then, I might have been bothered and freaked out. So I accepted that which he gave me. I know since then that they are not what he said they were. But he had said it in order not to scare me.

Frank looked at some kind of map and he told me, "You're not going to be worried. Don't worry anymore because you're going to be all right. The next five years everything's going to be really good for you." Actually, it took me a little more than five years to work out the karma in the condition that I was. It was altogether ten years, to be exact.

"Eventually you will end up in a hot country," Frank also said.

I said, "California?"

He wouldn't commit himself.

Then I said, "Well, if you're leaving, what's going to happen? Are you coming back for me?"

He said, "Yes, I'll be back for you."

"When will that be?" I wanted to know.

It was very difficult for him, as I recall, to figure out time. It really puzzled him.

I asked, "Is it five years? Is it ten years?"

He said, "I think it's five years."

I figured maybe it would be ten years, but now it's been fifteen years, and he still hasn't contacted me again. I have not heard from Frank in all this time.

Chapter 6

On My Own ... But Not Really

Frank left in September 1973. I knew him for about two years. He told me he had to go look after somebody else up north. After he left, I couldn't ask him about any more questions regarding my life.

The things he had told me were vivid in my memory. "Love is a requirement," he had said. "Love and understanding without judgment." Not to be judgmental. In other words, to be a child and to accept without hesitation. Remember one thing, when you have a certain vibration, people will come to you with that same vibration. People who are of a lower vibration will repay you. People of a higher vibration will have understanding. The worst part of realizing where people are at is when they reject you because of that. When they're not ready to accept what you've got to say, or at least to listen to you, they don't have to accept you, but just listen.

I am ready to embrace new ideas. Most people are not. I feel it is important to be able to work towards the 22nd, 23rd and 24th centuries. People who can do this are the people they are interested in. Our space brothers are interested in people who can embrace new ideas. That's another reason why they have chosen artists, writers, etc. These are the people that are open—people who realize, at least, that there is something more than just what is down here.

Frank also said that we could heal ourselves. By being negative you really make yourself ill. By being a part of the positive flow, the body naturally renews itself. It's constantly doing that. I have found some people who appear to be ageless. One example is a man I met from Paonia, Colorado, by the name of Julian Joyce. It was hard for me to believe that he was a man of 78 who will soon be 80. This is a vital man because he is so high on the spiritual ladder. I believe that's the essence. This is one thing that Frank stipulated, that there are people who are positive. He did say that I will be the most positive aspect and, as he said, that is a very important thing in accepting new ideas as well.

"Those who seek to limit their possibilities have lost themselves in the perceived world," Frank once told me. He was not too thrilled at the way various races and religions try to reach the Creator, which constitutes so many different names. "Actually, there is only one Creator," he said. People go to their various churches and synagogues, and while they're praying they make all kinds of promises. Then as soon as they come out, they go back to their natural state. They have not conquered the idea that they need to rise above their greed and desires. It's all right to have desires, of course, but look how they go about reaching them.

Another time he said, "A normal life can be obtained only by the mastery of the mind over the body." I don't think that means the body is necessarily bad. The body is an instrument to be used for good or bad.

"The divine soul is potentially capable of making the individual a whole and harmonious man" was another thing Frank said.

Frank was not thrilled about gurus. He felt that many of them were not being truthful. He stressed that anybody who writes a book and lies, or in any way tries to fool everybody by making false claims, will suffer the consequences. He was very adamant about that. A book is important, after all, because people believe what they read. It's so important to be truthful.

One time I went to Ferndale, Washington, which is between Bellingham and Blaine, to visit a friend who is since deceased. The two of us would go into meditation, and during this visit, after we had done some meditation, I showed her a small disc which Frank had given me a long time ago with my

"The World of Tomorrow through Imagination." A stairway to the beyond. Figures that are floating along playfully and incredible, alive, endowed with magical powers. A kaleidoscope in color, a range of various shapes, swirling lines depicting forever motion.

space name on it. Unfortunately, I have lost that disc. My friend touched the disc and she put it down quickly and said to me, "You're connected with space!" She was very psychic.

In our meditations we pulled in only high entities, from all different prophets—we even had Jesus—all the most important people coming to our meditation sessions. She could even see them.

One day while I was coming out of her house, I looked up at the sky and saw this gigantic man in the sky. I yelled at her, "Charlene! Come look!" She looked, and she also saw a man in the sky. That incident prompted my series of paintings, which includes my favorite painting, Man in the Sky.

Then I met Yonnish. He took all of my UFO books and he threw them into the ocean. He thought I was possessed by demons! I lived with this man for two and one half years. He was sweet one moment, and the next … All I can figure is that he must have had a schizophrenic personality. But I guess I had to go through all of that.

Then I begged to see how I could say goodbye to this

person. "Please, dear God," I prayed, "show me a way to say goodbye to him."

And the answer came. When I went to France for my art exhibit, I put all the little books I had on metaphysics and UFOs where he would think I had hidden them. Then when he saw those books, he picked me up at the airport and brought me to the house, where he packed up all of his things and left. In that way I didn't take away his manhood. He thought *he* was ending the relationship. He thought I would scream because I don't like sleeping alone or living alone. Well, I fooled him.

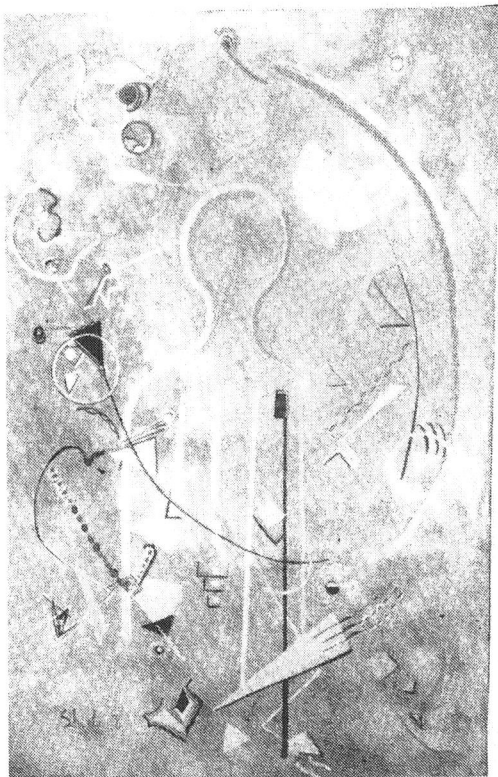

"The Man in the Sky" painting, inspired by what I and a friend saw.

For five years, while I was living in White Rock, I went through a difficult time, learning to live alone and sleep alone. Many nights I would sleep with an eye open. I was fulfilling the time when Frank said I had to stay where I was, and White Rock was very close to where Arne and I lived on the farm. It was like I was "doing time." It was hard for me to sleep. Apparently I had to work off some of my karma and this was one way I did it. I probably did one of my best paintings during this period, because I painted at night since I couldn't sleep. Little by little, I learned how to sleep by myself. Eventually the time came when I was strong. I even reached the point where I didn't want to move from White Rock, but then upstairs decided I had to.

In November 1978, Maureen, a psychic friend of mine, had a dream in which she was told I had to move to North Vancouver. "Tell Shirlè she must move to North Vancouver" were the instructions. This turned out to be a turning point in my life. I feel I was really guided to make this move because if I hadn't, I might not have met my husband Fred.

I moved from White Rock to North Vancouver. I was invited to a party one evening. It was a baby shower and a friend of mine wanted me to go with her. Since she lived in North Vancouver, she drove me, and she literally had to drag me to this party because I didn't want to go. After all, I didn't know the people. The daughter of a friend of hers was having the baby. The girl's parents were divorced, but both she and her ex-husband were at this party.

I was sitting in the living room between two other ladies when Fred Carsh, the pregnant girl's father, walked into the room and saw me. He immediately showed an interest in me and he went over to his ex-wife and asked about me. "Who is that woman sitting between Ann Spanner and Anne Niesen?"

His ex-wife laughed. "That's Shirlè Klein. Forget about her. She's an artist … a *crazy* artist … and she's poor as a church mouse."

That weekend there was a dance which I attended, and Fred Carsh came to that dance. I was surprised when he came directly over to me and asked me to dance with him. I did him a favor and accepted. After that he just would not leave my side. Following the dance, I went home and he went home, and I thought that was all there was to it.

Wrong! He called me up mid-week and asked me to marry him!

"You're absolutely crazy!" I told him. "I don't even know you."

And Fred said, "But I know you."

So I knew these were the words. I knew that I had to pay attention to whatever was going on because Frank had told me the man I would meet would *know* me and tell me so. The romance lasted awhile, but eventually I came to connect with and care for Fred, and we are now married.

In 1984, while I was going through a difficult time, I heard about a psychic fair from my art friends, and I decided I just had to go. I learned that on one of the days the psychic fair was going to have a lecture with photos and moving photographs of outer space and spacecraft. I wanted to go to that, to see what was happening. So I went.

As I was watching Dorothy Isaac show her photos, I felt the urge come over me that now was the time. It was intermission time and I said to myself, "My God, it's time *now.*" Up to this point I had been going along solo, minding my own business, not doing anything about what I had learned or knew. Suddenly I knew I had to do something about it. So I walked over to the gentleman giving the lecture. His name was Graham Conway. I said to him, "Mr. Conway, I think I have something that might interest you."

I showed him a little of the photos of the writing that I had, given to me by Frank. He got excited. He said he'd be very interested in seeing more, so I said, "Could you ask Dorothy and yourself to please come and I will show you something."

Well, Graham Conway called me up. He said Dorothy couldn't make it, but asked if he could bring a man who was an investigator from South Africa. I said, "Sure." They came at 8 p.m. and didn't leave until midnight. They were both very impressed with what I had to show them.

Then I got a letter from Aileen Edwards. "I hear that you've got some plates," she told me in the letter. At first I was upset, for the simple reason—*who's Aileen?* I didn't know who she was or what she was, but through meditation I got the answer that it would be all right to correspond with her. So I sent Aileen four of the photographs of four plates, and I got back an answer.

"There's a lady by the name of Helene," she wrote me, "and she deciphers plates. You have four more."

So I sent Aileen the other four, and then Helene telephoned me long distance from Arizona, where she was residing at the time. She said, "Listen, what you've got is so incredible!" Then she said, "I have to come up and see you because the last one is the most important plate of all. I just have to come and see you." Then she added, "And I feel towards you like you are my sister." This was the closeness Helene felt toward me.

When Aileen came up to visit me along with her husband Dan Edwards, I went through my story again and they were quite taken with the whole thing. After I was through with my story, I said, "And there are some things that I still cannot divulge. The time isn't right for that. That will have to be left for perhaps a future date, but right now I can't."

Dan cried, "But you've got to!"

"Dan," I said, "I'm not going to." And that was that.

Then Aileen met with someone in Vancouver whom she was hoping would try to start a group, a UFO Contact Center. She and Dan had founded UFO Contact Center International in June 1981, and were trying to get support centers started across the continent. I went along with her. For some reason the plan failed and this person did not start a center. Aileen turned to me and said, "I wish there was somebody here who would start a group."

Then a few people came over to me and said, "Shirlè, why don't you start a center?"

"Me? What do I know about organizations? Who says I know all about this ... I'm an artist. I don't have time for all that."

That night I went to bed and I had a strange dream. In the dream was a wild white horse that came running towards me. I stopped the horse and quietened it. Suddenly, there was a door that opened, and there standing in the doorway was the Lion from *The Wizard of Oz*, who needed courage. He wanted courage, and he turned around and there was a handle. I grabbed the handle and the mane of the horse, then the reins, and I went through that door.

From that dream I knew that I had to have courage and

In the dream
the lion looked
like Bert Lahr.

WIZARD OF OZ *stars Bert Lahr as the cowardly lion, just one of the film's memorable characters.*

start the group, so I started the group. I had asked, and the answer came to me that it was time to do it, and so I did it. It was 1984 when I became an associate director of UFO Contact Center International. That first year was the one in which we were gung-ho. I started out by holding meetings in my little house, and at the first meeting there were sixty people. I continued to hold meetings in my home for a short while until we couldn't take it any longer. I decided we had to get other places in which to hold our meetings.

We got a place that was on top of a high elevated building. It was right close to the stars, which was appropriate for us. We had that place for a solid year, and we had the most incredible meetings there. It was a cinch to get people to speak at that time. After four years, we are still going strong. I won the award for Best Associate Director twice, which was presented at Jorpah, which is UFO Contact Center's annual gathering. The word *Jorpah* comes from an alien word meaning gathering from Greta Woodrew's book, *A Slide of Light*. Every fall people gather from around the world for a weekend of interesting lectures and fellowship, the topic being—of course—UFOs.

Making the commitment and being an associate director of UFO Contact Center International sometimes means standing up to criticism in public. I was on a TV show in Nelson. I called up Aileen and told her I was going to be on the show and I thought at the time, "Gee, it would be nice if Aileen could be on the show with me." Well, I had another meeting and Aileen came to it. I asked her if there was any chance she could go to Nelson with me.

"When are you going to Nelson?" she asked.

I said, "On the 9th."

She said, "What do you mean? I'm going to be there." So we got to do the show together.

Whenever I go somewhere, I hand out various things from my little UFO folder. I was talking at the Metric Conversion in spring of 1987 and I spoke to about one hundred people. I was practically crucified at that meeting. One lady got up.

There were many different kinds of people there. They were all different. There were metaphysical views on reincarnation, someone spoke on the Buddhist religion, etc. There were actually quite a few of us talking on UFOs. My talk centered around how interesting it was that even TV shows are picking up on UFOs as well, and that—despite the cover-up—people feel there is something more going on.

One woman, after I finished my speech and had asked for questions, got up and asked a question. After I responded, another lady got up and started screaming at me and saying that I had come from the devil, and so forth. I very nicely let her scream and finish her screaming, and then I said to her, "I want to tell you something. I wouldn't be here if I thought this was the devil's work."

So again she yelled at me. "But you could be an ignorant party!"

I shook my head. "No," I told her. "Ignorance is a sin, and I'm not ignorant in that department."

Later I found out this lady knew someone who knew me, and got hold of the whole story about my background, and then she felt quite badly about her outbursts.

I've had to undergo all the metamorphosis and let go of all the accustomed religion, the whole thing, in order to reach the level where I am, and yet—funny the way it is—I still go to synagogue. I still take part in that, although it doesn't really touch me, actually. I'm just a part of that group.

I can accept anything if it doesn't change my thinking, or if it doesn't change the way that I feel. I would like to feel that I can go anywhere, that I can walk into a Christian church, or into a Buddhist temple. I want to be free to go everywhere. I don't want to have to say, "No, that's taboo," or "This I shouldn't do." I don't want this *shouldn't do*. What is here on this Earth I want to know about, to experience, and I feel I'm strong enough to have the belief system of what is good. Once I am told "You must not do that!"—rest assured I will *do* it, because no one has the right to tell me until I myself am strong enough to make up my own mind, to direct my own thinking.

Otherwise I wouldn't have been given this job. That would mean I could very easily be misled. They don't have time for people who are very easily led or misled. As my contact said, I'm a rebel. I've always been a rebel. He told me many of the people that they had contacted have somehow ended up in psychiatric wards or in mental institutions because they could not differentiate one thing from another. I guess that's why they came to me in the flesh, so to speak, because of the importance of this job. If they had come to me as an illusion or something, I would have put it down as such. Of all the incredible dreams I have had, that's exactly what I do think of them—as dreams. So if they have this important job for me to do, and Frank had to wait around to help me with my karmic conditions and all the things that I had to work out, he would have to be in the physical.

It was June of 1986 and I wasn't feeling well. In fact, I hadn't been feeling well for quite a while. For two years my back had been giving me problems. I didn't have a lot of pain at first, but I kept falling. I went to a doctor, a specialist, and he did a CT scan and discovered I had arthritis of the spine, of two of the vertebrae, and also a slipped disc. I really suffered a lot.

I decided to ask for help from the people upstairs. I told them if they couldn't help me, I would still do their work for them. No matter how much pain I suffered, I would do the work anyway.

Well, that evening they sent someone to help me. I was in a miserable state. Finally I went to bed, not caring if I ever walked again. I was tired of falling. I just didn't care anymore. With this attitude I fell asleep.

I had been sleeping when suddenly I heard a sneeze. So I woke up. In front of me, standing by my bed, was a not-very-tall, slim man who was bending over my legs. He wore some sort of a costume, and he reminded me of Danny Kaye with the mass of curly hair. The hair was a very light shade of green, and he wore almost like an artist's smock. He had on brown woolly pants. For some reason I thought of him as being a fairy, but he was actually of regular height. He just stood there, bending over my knees. He waited until I had fully recovered from my state of sleep, and then he simply disappeared.

My first thought was one of relief. Thank goodness, they had sent someone to help! Then I discovered I could not get out of bed. It was even worse than before! "Well, thank you very much!" I cried in exasperation. This went on for two more weeks, and then one day I got off the bed with no more pain. It was five days before my birthday—the most welcome birthday present I've ever received.

I did not know that they had reconstructed my spine until I wrote to my friend in Paris, who did a séance to find out about what had transpired. They said that the curly-haired man was a healer from another planet, that he had reconstructed my spine. I haven't had any more problems. As a matter of fact, the doctor, the specialist that I went to with my problem, could not believe what had happened.

It was 1987 when I met the shaman. This shaman, who lives in Curve Lake, Peterborough, Ontario, came looking for me the first time. He apparently travels to other planets. He was told to look for two ladies—one by the name of Shirlè, and the other one by the name of Helene.

Through the grapevine he was in contact with a friend of mine, Jean-Pierre, and Jean-Pierre told him that Helene doesn't live here—Helene lives in Arizona—but that Shirlè lives here. So the shaman finally got to me and his first message was to me, "Get ready to be moving." That was in 1987. I still haven't moved yet. Apparently they warn you first, and it takes a year or two before everything happens. Well, when the shaman came to me the second time, the answer this time was that it was up to me.

Getting back to the first time he contacted me, he related that they were very, very pleased with me, of what I was doing, and to continue on with what I was doing. That was the message. Since I didn't know who he was, to have him suddenly come to me was a surprise in itself.

Then it was July 1987. I was supposed to go and visit a friend who was in the hospital. I didn't feel like going. I had gotten up that morning and I told Fred, "I don't know why, but I've got to go to the hospital to visit my friend." Then I added, "But I don't feel well."

Fred said, "What's the matter with you?"

I said, "I don't know."

I went into my study and—bingo—here comes the call from the shaman. I said to him, "What are you doing in town? What's happening?"

"I've got to see you," he said.

"Isn't that funny?" I replied. "I wanted to go somewhere but ..."

"I know," he said, "we stopped you. I've got to see you *now*."

So I got into my car to go to The Market. He took the sky train to The Market. When we met, he had all kinds of things to tell me. "You've got to go," he said. "You're going to Nelson."

"What?" I cried. "Who told you?"

"Never mind who told me," he said. "You've got to go. You're going to Nelson."

"What for?"

"You need a tone."

This puzzled me.

"You're going to see this lady," he explained. "Her name is Celeste."

"Fine," I said, and wrote down her name.

"She'll give you a note—a tone," he told me. "We can't help you do the things that you have to do unless you are healed."

"Why? What's wrong with me?" I persisted.

The shaman pointed to his breast. "Because from up here you are having problems." He was referring to my heart. "And this tone will help you," he insisted. "It's a healing tone."

I said, "Fine."

"Oh ... and there's one more thing," he said. "We've decided to give you carte blanche."

The shaman explained that because I was worthy and had control—I didn't desire things just for myself—I had earned the right and they had decided to give me carte blanche on the spiritual level.

"Everything and anything," he explained, "that you want to do ... go ahead and do it, and we'll back you. Whatever you say and whatever you want, just anything and everything ... "

"But why?"

"We have that much faith in you." And then he gave me a message for Helene, which I wrote down and sent on to Helene in Arizona. I had told him I wanted to intercede for Helene, in order to help her out, and he said I should not intercede for anyone. Yet he gave me the message, which had a lot to do with the Indian way, as in a parable. Helene's life *did* change because of the message. So, in some roundabout way, I did succeed at helping her.

I went to Nelson and had an art show. I was supposed to speak at the university in Nelson, and they advertised my talk on TV, but it didn't get broadcast. Apparently some Christian bookstore decided to show a camp video instead. When the person who had arranged for me to come called up the TV station to report that something had gone wrong, and why wasn't my speech on the air, he got the runaround. "Something's broken and we can't turn it off!"

Funny how the moment I left everything was okay again. I believe someone was fearful of what I had to say and prevented it from being aired. Nevertheless, there were about twenty people at my lecture who were interested in what I had to say and were themselves interesting people.

When I telephoned Celeste Crowley and asked if she could see me, she turned me down. "I'm really busy," she said.

"But listen," I told her, "the space brothers told me to

come and see you."

After a short pause she said, "Okay, come over right away."

So I went to her house. She explained she had been channeling lately, that something had been happening to her, and she was seeing aliens.

I reassured her by saying, "Well, they think so much of you. They sent me to you to give me a tone."

Then we went into meditation and she did some healing ritual using crystals and the chakras. She used a rose quartz on me. Then, finally Celeste said to me, "Pick yourself out a tone."

I did. I randomly picked out the G tone. I found out then that G is for the heart. And the heart was where I was having problems. I don't understand how I happened to pick out that particular tone. All I did was open my mouth and sing, "Ahhh …" and it was the note, G.

Needless to say, I was healed. Two days later was my birthday, and Celeste sent me the rose quartz she had used on me. I thought that was a very sweet gesture on her part.

Of the many people I have met, there was one particular person in Nelson who was so affected by my lecture that I became instrumental in her progress. We have been in contact with each other ever since. Perhaps she may be our next associate director of UFO Contact Center International.

Chapter 7

Interpretation of the Ten Plates

This chapter consists of Helene's interpretation of the 10 plates she was forced to memorize as a child.

PLATE I

I am to all creatures of void, mass and life; I am the protector from time eternal, past and future travel by my subjects to all my creation, save and renewed, the place of peace. Many prophets I have touched from stars and the galaxies and this earth to protect my emissary from the wrath of negative forces. Only the unity of all mankind will survive the wrath of the one that has been raped and plundered. Hear my word, human of the universe. Join in harmony to form a positive force when the galaxies that I have assembled with pride has come to its own destiny. Help your brothers and its humanity to survive the change that man has inflicted on himself. Prepare all touched ones to leave until the light returns. The craft that you made is the means of salvation for these nations. Leave this galaxy. Instruct your people, teach them the way of the light and the knowledge. Return them to their origins as this is imperative. Remove direction controls as they are able to guide themselves in peace and harmony. Protector and healer; stay with them until they have found the healing from within. Place all knowledge of you in their energies. Leave them the craft of salvation for they are now one with me, of me. These are my directions and my love.

PLATE I.2

I am the light and the direction. I have chosen among you the traveler. I have guarded you from the black force. We are the light, the power and love. I have chosen your tribe to help and protect all that is human. The time has come to assist once again, human and Earth.

Choose wisely—the unity for our experiment has failed. Assemble your light and power and reclaim our chosen ones.

Guide them to the land of the Twelve Peaks. On each continent they will be assembled. Direct your Earth brother to form their circles so that they may search and draw close all the humans of light. Turn your head to the North as your human heart may lead you in the wrong direction. The time is short. Do not bring along spoiled fruit for they have contaminated their own existence and that of others. Walk in the light, keep your spirit looking up, confer with your council.

The protectors will guide the six directors as the light touches you. You will no longer be female or male but human. Do not forget the past, find in your tribes the seven knowledges that is the key to the sound of the trumpet. Follow the sound that directs all humanity. Find the crystal that will not break for that is the guide to awaken the two lights of energy who have been waiting the release for action to return to the infinite. The trial is complete. The Council with "I AM" will guide them to me in the light.

PLATE II

I am the power and the light. From the smallest one to the greatest, none will fear my wrath as was once felt. I cleanse your Earth and I promise humanity this will never happen again, but as the Creator of all the universe, I have sent emissaries to help me in my work. They have searched to find the subjects that are of our flesh. Everything is in readiness. Now the time has come to leave behind all that is material for I have provided for you. Fear not this journey. The staff of life is with you. Look high on the mountain of the Seven Peaks. The rest will follow my command and my directions.

PLATE II.2

All you, my people, work together as the time is now to accomplish all that must be done. The little one named USO will come to help and show you your capabilities. Do not fear him, as he is good and understanding. Negative forces that have made your Earth what it is have even created a false prophet and from the East he will control many masses. Turn your head away. Do not let him touch you as you will lose all the power and strength that will be bestowed upon you. In your devotion for the cause you will be protected from the fungus. All of these, my people, is to assure you that I have cared for your destiny. Do not weaken. Find the eagle who carries the red cloth in his talons!

PLATE III

You and all of yours will seek and relocate in the Valley of the 7 Peaks, for there you will be protected. Many changes are upon you. There you will find the house of Mother Earth. Do not believe all that you will see there, it will be but an illusion. The direction has the way to penetrate the entrance, but only when Brother Moon will peer through the view hole will you see the secret of the pivot. Push gently and enter for you have been worthy. If there may be an unworthy one with you, you will be refused at the entrance. It could mean your physical death. Remember your high level of consciousness is the learning of all the Earth possesses. Return alone. Meditate until you are worthy of facing that which is greater than your being. Go with peace in your heart.

PLATE III.2

You must leave behind the physical, the earthly and mundane acquisition. For the light infinite will provide all that your being requires. Take with you only your science and knowledge. The path to the rendezvous is clear to the ones that have been touched. The teacher, the tradesman, the healer, the being that has the courage and the love of their destiny will all be greeted with life and love.

Find along your travel the rock of eternal life and the crystal that will sing to the glory of a new life. Beware of bringing with you the negative energies for they will make your travel difficult and perilous and at the end they will be turned away. Again, I say, do not look back at the blanket of darkness that covers the place which you came from. Look to the light and the sound of the call. Let not what you see distract you of your destiny.

PLATE IV

I am the unity that guided you. A place has been chosen for you. The truth will accompany you. My writing has laid dormant until now. Many millenniums have passed since my hand dictated these words for you. All of you have made many gods. They have come and gone for they were not the real gods. I have given you all the tools to prepare my arrival but you have chosen to create your own destruction. I come to you once again, as you have lost the love I have so many times taught you. My chosen children have been suppressed and their knowledge gone astray. Now I will give you my directions. Follow them as humanity depends on it.

PLATE IV.2

The only god you should worship is the one of the infinite, for he has made all the universe and its life forms. We are but his creation. No one can duplicate his masterpiece. We are the greatest of his creation. The time has come to elevate all our energies to meet the creation that have traveled so far from the distant galaxy. The infinite join with them your mind and energies for they are there to help you acquire the knowledge to survive your ordeal. Go with them so that you can learn from them to rebuild your Earth into the paradise that it once was.

PLATE V

I am the direction and the light, all that have been touched must prepare supplies for the bodies and soul must be guarded. The time is short and the season foul for the time is upon us. Leave the city. Change your dwelling. Do not make it of wood as they will also be destroyed. Surround your tribes. Name your guardian, not your leader. The trial and tribulation will make you find peace and contentment. Keep away from the large bodies of water. Reserve a room for all that is perishable, and place there a protector. Do not search to do this. Let it be a unity project. Leave the city to the unworthy, for they will be their own destruction. Go to the Valley of Twelve Peaks. It is the place to wait the coming of your new life. Preserve all that you bring with you of the past. The past is your heritage. All who travel show the young ones the horror that man has created on this beautiful planet so they do not repeat your wicked ways. My word must remain your guidance and your peace.

PLATE V.2

I am your guide and your light, follow this guideline as it is but a guide. My grace will wrap you during your travel. One has been chosen on all of your continents so that all will be in readiness just for you. The time and water will not be a reason to keep you apart. My guidance will bring you together.

The star that appears is the guide that will take you to the place of gathering. Arrange what life is left to you to gather all that must come. Do not try to persuade as those are not of your tribe. Greed and ego is a pitfall, guard yourself from them. It is time to form your council, wait no more. The star that all have sought has been found. It is with us. Beware of false snakes for their venom will poison you and make you lose your way. Keep to the simplicity, the more the wealth the more the danger. You must find your other self for he also is looking. Tell to all this message for only a few will respond. The strength is always with you. (Mikawus) The high one will come to you. Peace and love eternal.

PLATE VI

I am justice for all the universes. The subjects are in waiting, the time is upon us when the sun and the moon is in totalities and the earth is in darkness. The time for the touched ones to assemble, two by two, the guardian will direct all the marked ones.

The travelers carry with them all the instruction to guard us against the pilferer of other galaxies. They are many, but the light and the truth will recognize their dark powers. Long have we waited for these times. Beware of the teller of tales for he cannot look you in the eye. The travel of energy gather with force, few are in view. The place where the points meet will be the window of the future. The flame of all mystery, when the water cleans away all of the decay, the safe place will be protected by the energy. Look to the sky. Search there for the Mother of Salvation.

PLATE VI.2

I am with you to guide you though many seasons will come and go. The wise one will have the knowledge and foresight to go where the trees are many. Beware of the one that was not marked, for he will be the taker of breath. He will dig his talon in your mind until it will pass beyond. My justice is for all, it will speak only once.

Protect the young with your cloth of energy. When the sky is red and the water of brine boils with the cry of millions, turn your eyes away and see only with your mind for then the protector will ring the sound that will reach around the terra, and the great change will take place.

PLATE VII

I am the voice of the past, present and future. I have listened since the beginning of your galaxy. The knowledge of all human race I have given you to make your world a bond with your Earth. I have returned again after millennium to find decays of the human race. The powers entrusted to you are wasted in degradation, except for a few who remain true. Again my brothers have come to help by giving you knowledge to avoid the total destruction of your planet. We have a large vessel beneath your surface, set there with protectors who are waiting the signal of the sound that crumbles and moves the ground.

The mind is free to elevate and join the many. All will come to the point of the crystal long ago. Traces were made to bring the Mothers safely. Marks and direction have been erased. Close your eyes and speak not. Walk without stumbling for the earth will convulse. Trace the aura. You are one, you are many.

PLATE VII.2

I will guide you through the passage that all must experience. The black force will dare my light only to be terminated. Set aside all that you have touched and encircle your loved ones for we are all one.

The air that surrounds you has been made foul from above. Dig into the earth after it has stopped trembling.

The maker of the earth's law and its government shall destroy their very own existence for they were warned but did not care for their greed led them to destroy all that they stood for. Not one nation will be at peace when the great sound is heard. Many false leaders will try to restore the upheaval. They will all fall for their lack of unity and guidance. They will burn in the heat from the sun. The cry of humanity will be heard throughout the planet, but the brothers will fill the winds with sleep for all who remain.

PLATE VIII

I am the light and the direction when the black ashes covers your world. To all that are marked, direct and guide humanity on your continent. The point of pivot and balance will be there where I will guide all the chosen children who will have survived the sickness of man's corruption of the air that you breathe. These children are the energy of tomorrow.

The infernal machine of war will be released by the greedy ones; all will lose.

On each continent I have guided one soul, one brother, one sister, to tell of the places that the flame of the sky won't reach. Protect these areas as they are the point of salvation. Learn the energies of the sun, wind, and the hot earth. Do all that the protector instructs you. Raise your mind and spirit. Become in balance with what is left of your Earth. Waste not precious time with tears of the past, for both are weakness. Find strength in the knowledge that you are one.

PLATE VIII.2

I am the direction and guardian of all that is in the universe. All that I have created man has destroyed.

My messenger has come in peace to teach you to survive man's destruction. Find the grains that grow in the ground with man's energy. Reap the harvest from the earth for beast and sea fruit, there will be no more.

Learn to sustain the nations from what can be planted inside of the dome, where the light will fortify and surmount the negative flashes that is man's mistake.

I now give you the coordinates that you will follow to start a new generation. Beware of the one who has turned a deaf ear to these words, for he will come upon you like a mad dog. Use the light to protect yours.

LATITUDE	LONGITUDE
A ...... 30 degrees 44 minutes	...... 114 degrees 37 minutes
N ...... 31 degrees 08 minutes	...... 111 degrees 40 minutes
M ...... 35 degrees 03 minutes	...... 106 degrees 37 minutes
...... 35 degrees 39 minutes	...... 105 degrees 58 minutes
U ...... 40 degrees 46 minutes	...... 111 degrees 53 minutes
...... 41 degrees 15 minutes	...... 111 degrees 57 minutes
C ...... 38 degrees 49 minutes	...... 105 degrees 08 minutes
...... 40 degrees 00 minutes	...... 104 degrees 31 minutes

PLATE IX

I am you and your brother. Your directions are clear. Go forward and touch the spirit of many but do not confuse mysticism, white or black magic or charlatanry for the words that come from within. Be true to your peers and above all, to yourself. Each touched one must stand out from the one that pretends for that one is lost to eternity. Grow in your mind. Raise yourself above the highest level of consciousness. Feel with your heart but remain humble, for this humility will advance you in my esteem. With your mind you will achieve what man has tried and failed. When the great trauma shakes the entire earth and cities crumble, in your safe zone your fate will be re-enforced. The great sound will ring but once.

PLATE IX.2

I who prepare every energy, who is soul, beware of the vendors for their trickery is empty. Many more messengers will make themselves known from the four corners of the earth. They will gather. Look into their eyes for the signal, for it is in all of them. Soon the financial establishment will drown in their own mountain of corruption. The government will be chaotic. The military will have no leaders. At this point Mother Nature will rumble and separate this continent. Every unclean one will be lost in their short coming. Listen in your mind for the sound of survival.

PLATE X

I am the one to turn to; not as a religion, not as a god, but as yourself. The light has guided you in the direction of the truth. Keep with you my command and salvation will be yours. The first monument to fall will be that of all churches, as they cultivate fear and ignorance. Turn to your creator for he has written his commandment in your heart, not in a book. Do not make a religion of the space brothers. Their level is one with the eternal light. They are of flesh and blood, the same as you. For a millennium they have elevated their level of consciousness. Work with them, for they are fighting the battle of space, the same as you on Earth. The black power is everywhere. The negative is a strong force.

PLATE X.2

I am the greatness in all of the chosen ones. Gather together all the knowledge I have given you, for the time is near. Some of you will travel from afar with very little worldly possessions. The spirit that will guide you will be the power within you. The light and the truth will sustain you. The ship will await you. You will find there your likeness, in a new time. Upon your return, the earth will welcome new pioneers. You will have come from which you started, your knowledge completed.

PEACE AND LIGHT TO ALL CREATURES

Chapter 8

Instrument of the Cosmic Spirit

I have never had M.I.B. experiences. The M.I.B., or the Men in Black, are notorious in UFO literature for harassing people who have had contact with aliens. I feel the M.I.B. is the government. I believe this because whenever anybody has had an experience in which they have been given something, these people come in and take it away, or they threaten that person with his or her life.

Space people don't have to go to all that trouble. They *contact* you. Why would they send someone out to tell you, "Don't you dare tell this and that …"? That's stupid, in my opinion. What is there for them to gain? Space people would merely say, "Let them go and talk. They won't be believed anyway." It's the government that is creating all this harassment, and the people need to know about how other people are being harassed.

As my contact told me, "Anybody who has any ill thinking about you, or wants to hurt you … we will look after it." So if anyone would want to come to me and harm me, they would forget all about it. For instance, they might come to my door but suddenly not remember where they were or why. I am not worried about them. I know they will not touch me.

One time an evil entity came to me. He took a cushion while I was in bed, placed it on top of me and tried to smother me. I just very nicely surrendered. I said, "God, if that's your will, that's fine with me." Then the entity vanished. I suppose that was another test. You see, we're always tested by our faith.

You can say you have a lot of faith, but let some threatening incident come into being—and how strong is your faith then? So every now and then I was tested. I am not tested anymore because I have *carte blanche.* What's the use of their testing me if I come out the winner anyway? So they are through testing me. I have the faith. They know exactly what I am willing to do.

Interdimensional beings are with us all of the time. I once had an artist friend who lived next door to me in White Rock, on the ocean. One day he was looking out at the ocean when he suddenly saw transparent people. When he told me he had seen transparent people, I started making transparent paintings. He was stunned. He saw these people. They were digging something. It couldn't be water. They were digging on another level some place. He obviously had pierced the veil to get a glimpse at another dimension. At first he thought, "Something's wrong with my eyes," so he walked away into the other room. Then he turned back around and, sure enough, they were still there. He said this lasted for a good half hour.

Here is another example of a different dimension. One day I simply turned around and saw a woman asleep on my bed. I found out then that we get glimpses every now and then of an interdimensional level. There's not only heaven and earth, but within and without, and many levels in between. When the veil is parted, it's just a lucky moment when certain people experience it. Maybe that person was once in that dimension and maybe they are prone to that dimension. There are so many reasons why some people seem to have the ability to see different dimensions.

I remember once watching a television program that disturbed me so much that I was in tears. I went to bed and, all of a sudden, I awoke and saw the archangel Michael, with his wings spread out to protect me.

I have heard some people tell about the strangest creatures coming at night to view them while they sleep. I, too, have had some very strange and—by the ordinary standards, some very ugly—creatures come towards me. I don't seem to get them anymore, but I used to. From the artist's point of view, however, they are very beautiful, even though they are grotesque. I told them, "God, you're so beautiful!" They looked startled and disappeared. I think they, too, require love. This whole process of interdimensional, multidimensional, spatial dimensional—everything—all runs on love. *They, too, require love!* Everything and everybody requires it.

In my life I have had some amazing dreams. I used to dream about earthquakes. One day after I had dreamed about an earthquake which really disturbed me, I went to my contact and told him about it. After the earthquake, I had seen gold flakes falling down. Frank said to me, "Well, that's probably the Golden Age. What will take place is ... the old will be shattered away." Then he explained, "It wasn't the earthquake *per se,* but the soul speaking to you. The old will fall away, and this will be the Golden Age, to build on." Then he continued. "And of course there will be difficulty. There will be a lot of resistance from the born-again Christians and the formal religions. They're frightened of that because in some ways it's a whole new concept." Then he added, "We take responsibility for ourselves. We don't submerge ourselves as a group, but we take the responsibility ourselves."

I remember being with President Jimmy Carter once in a dream. Another time I was at one of the banquets with the Fords, and I was sitting and talking at their table. I dreamed about being with various big figures and discussing politics with them. I think that happens when a person is dreaming. Somehow your vibrations cross with that other person, and you know each other personally—or your souls do, at least. You see, we all know each other, really. It's just conscious role-playing that we go through, and this role-playing blocks out everything. If you were to remember, you most likely would not be playing the role that you are playing right now.

Fred has had some fantastically weird dreams as well. He's always dreaming of flying. One night he dreamt he was flying.

He flew up to a large building and then was asked to do some work on that building. He told me the dream was so interesting. They had some new process that he was performing. He said that he was putting some things together that he had never seen before.

And then, in another dream Fred had, he was flying on the wings of an airplane. There was a whole city being carried along. The electricity in the city was on and the people were there, just flying along with it. They had just picked up a whole city. He saw that and he asked them how they were able to do that. They explained to him all in very technical terms, which I don't understand, but Fred does. He was pretty impressed by that dream.

Fred is becoming more open-minded. He has had so many different kinds of experiences on his own that he should probably write a book of his own. He experienced three or four wars. He had to leave Germany at the age of fifteen. His father was killed by the Nazis. His sister was put in a concentration camp, and his mother went into hiding in a convent. He's had things happen to him that are absolutely astounding.

The day Fred and I got married, he saw a man's face in a big blue bubble floating over to him. I believe it was probably Hymie giving his approval. Fred claims it was a dream, but he doesn't know for sure. He might have been awake when he saw that. Although he was really impressed by the experience, I didn't know what to make of it.

I feel Fred is being looked after in many ways because Fred is an extremely high technical individual. He's also an inventor. My husband is a very gifted man and they show him things. He comes up with things that are mind-boggling. He now accepts much of the UFO phenomenon, but at first he would say, "I really don't believe that." He had to see it to believe it, he used to claim. He had to have the experience or else he simply wasn't going to bother with it. So many people have this attitude.

I would tell Fred, "If you don't believe, it's not going to

happen ... whatever it is. If you believe, then it will happen. They don't have time for people who are non-believers. There are too many *believers* around."

It is my belief that UFOs are people—maybe space people—or they are our tomorrows. We are heading in that direction. Evolution has a way of going through various different cycles. The space people tell us they have gone through various different cycles. The space people tell us they have gone through all of that. The spirituality of an individual continues on the same path as evolution. All these new things coming out about space people are for *our time*—now. Who knows? A hundred years from now there may be another kind of people because we're forever evolving.

I have never thought of them as gods. Neither do I stand in awe of them. As a matter of fact, when my contact showed me all these things that were so incredible, I didn't gasp or show alarm. I took it all as being natural. My reaction was "Fine, you've got the technology ... you know as to what, but you were probably a hundred years ago back to where we are today." That's why I often tell my group not to stand in awe. Understand one thing—that you, too, are getting there—that you, too, are evolving.

The most important thing a human being should do in life is work on his or her spirituality. It is important to confront oneself and say, "Okay, I'm a little jealous of this person." Find out why. Understand that this person has reached their level and they are doing certain things. If you are jealous of that person, work yourself up to get to that level. Just say "good luck" to that person and be on your way.

When the common person sees a UFO, the purpose in seeing it is to awaken them. That's what happened to me when the two space people appeared in front of my bed. I probably would have had all these dreams about space, but I didn't connect the both of them. When you leave your body, you are a totally different individual.

Have you ever heard somebody say that they give lip

movement to something and years later they do it? If we *know* something, it's because we have already been doing it somewhere else. For example, I got a call from somebody I knew who said, "Oh gee, Shirlè, thanks very much for teaching me how to do eyes in one of my paintings."

"What are you talking about?" I said. "I haven't seen you in about a year."

"Oh," she said, "we were both up on Venus and—as a matter of fact—what kind of mural are you working on now?"

"How do you know I'm doing a mural?"

"Because you've just finished one up there. What are you doing?"

And I explained what it was to her.

"Yeah, you've done that up there," she said. So, without my knowing about it, she was telling me that I had shown her how to do certain things. She said, "You're teaching all the time, don't you know that?"

Apparently my soul goes and teaches and does other things, but the Shirlè personality doesn't know about it. The individual is a many-faceted person.

I no longer go looking for UFOs. I see some, but I simply don't go looking for them, and I'll tell you why. It's because it would mean I have lessened my faith that they are there. I would like to see them. When they think that I should, then I may see them. It's really not important to me anymore that I see them because I *know*. But whenever I'm with someone, they might appear. Then it's as if they're saying, "Hi, we're here."

When I take an airplane trip, I have a certain belt that I wear, given me by my contact, which is a material aspect for the character Shirlè to have. But for the soul Shirlè, it doesn't require that because she knows. However, for the personality that's playing Shirlè right now, it has its purpose. The belt contains certain magnets which cannot be seen. It takes a special instrument to detect them. I happen to know a person who has such an instrument, and he just tells me, "Don't leave home without it." It may sound like a credit card slogan, but I wear it practically all the time because I feel it's important to do so.

The belt is also another reason why I am not supposed to put on any more weight. My contact had told me that I have a tendency to gain weight and that I had better watch it. Apparently they have a suit ready for me, black with gold, and the belt is supposedly my gauge. If I cannot wear the belt, it's a sign that I had better start losing weight or I will get reprimanded.

Sometimes I am aware that I'm in contact with an alien person who will sit beside me in an airplane. Other times they may be with me somewhere just in case—like my contact said—if anything should happen to the plane. They would beam down that plane, he told me. So, if they can't get a spacecraft and they know I have to be somewhere, they will send an alien who will help in some way. I am able to sense that.

There are times when objects or individuals vanish before my eyes. I will come in somewhere and I'll say, "Ah-ha! What have we got here?" or I'll see something ... and *poof!* It's not there anymore. Fine. That means "Okay, I'm ready to accept everything." It's like a knowing. I have this knowing and I accept it as long as it's for the good. I will not accept anything that is for evil. I will fight tooth and nail. I will stand up for the underdog in every way possible because I don't like when an underdog's being hurt, whether he deserves it or not—that's none of my business. I have got to be there. In other words, I am a voice that has to be heard, and I'll stand up to the commitment.

Gabriel Greene visited me once in 1986. He lives out in Yucca Valley and Ashtar Command comes through to him. We were sitting around and talking when suddenly he did these gyrations. He told us, "Don't get excited. Don't get worried. I get all this because Ashtar wants to put somebody into space."

We asked, "Who?" There were eight of us present besides Gabriel.

"They want to put Shirlè into space," came the reply.

I said, "I'm ready." So I sat quietly and I honestly *saw* the space dome.

Gabriel said, "Okay, enter it."

So, in my way I entered it. I went through a whole series of what I saw in that spacecraft. I came to the conclusion that it was so beautiful, I thought for a moment it might be *my* spacecraft. But I don't know how valid that is. Being an artist, I always say, "Is it my imagination?" My whole problem is, if I didn't have such a vivid imagination, then maybe I would say, "Even though I see it, how much of it is imagination, and how much is reality?" You've got to be mad not to think that. I question it. I even question it when being regressed as well, because as I speak I *see* things. I am a visual person.

Shirlè the personality has to feel the person. I have to walk into the spacecraft myself and touch it, and then I'll know. That's true because I've had a lot of things which I have experienced, such as picking up the cart with my paintings on it. I *know* that I experienced that. I *know* it. I carried the paintings on one finger. I carried them! If I would have dropped them, they would have been carried anyway. Shirlè the personality experienced that. I felt inside and experienced it.

I had a brush with Shirley MacLaine in 1988. I received a call from a member of my group, Leia Andrews, and she told me, "Guess what? Shirley MacLaine is coming to Vancouver to view her show, *Madame Sousatska*." That was her new movie at the time. "She's coming to Vancouver," Leia continued, "and we've got to get a note to her."

"Leia, do you really feel strongly about this?" I asked.

"Yes, I do!"

"Do me a favor, Leia. I have so many things going on right now. You write the note and tell her a little about me."

So Leia wrote the note. Friday night came. I left Fred and went to meet Leia for dinner. Afterwards, we tried to get into the movie, but the show was closed. It was by invitation only. Naturally, we didn't have invitations. We didn't know the right people. Wouldn't you know—the ones that *should* be there were not there. The same old story.

Then I said to upstairs, "Okay, what is this all about?"

Then, who did I see but a friend of mine, Gary Pogrow, who writes for various plays and movies. I looked at him and said, "Gary? Is that really Gary?" Then I called to him.

"Shirlè?"

"Gary," I said, "are you going in to see Shirley MacLaine?"

"Yes," he said, "I have an invitation, don't you?"

I said no. "How do I know anybody to get me an invitation?" Then I said, "Can you do me a favor?" I thrust the note into his hand. "Give this note to her."

After he left, Leia said to me, "Do you think she'll get it?"

I said, "If it's meant to be, it's meant to be. I'm not going to worry about it."

We were walking in another direction when I saw Gary again. He was going to her closed party and he said, "Listen, Shirlè, I couldn't get it to her. There were too many people."

"Listen, Gary," I said, "give it to one of her entourage. She'll probably get it. If it's meant to be, she'll get it."

He sighed. "Well, if not ... should I give it back to you?"

"Just get it to her. Period."

"Okay," he said, "okay, don't get excited, I'll get it to her."

Sometime later I received a letter from Shirley MacLaine— actually from her publicity secretary—which said that Shirley MacLaine had asked her to write to me, that she was very happy I had given her the note, that she was now on a tour with her movie. "But she wanted me to tell you that she's glad you connected with her."

We are all instruments through the cosmic spirit. It's a whole life plan and everybody who wants to be an instrument can gladly be an instrument. I feel this is an opportunity not just open to a few. I hate it when somebody talks about "the few gifted" in referring to psychic people. We are all gifted. It's a choice you make. You want to help. You want to do things, so you are being helped to do things. If you want to do things and get rid of all your anger and your antagonism and your jealousies and your pettiness ... my dear God, the whole world is open to you.

This is what I feel people should understand. I hate the word *chosen*. It means a select group and that's it. Well, there's no such thing. The word *chosen* could be that you have decided that you yourself *chose* to do a specific thing. But then, everybody is! That's the mistake that people don't understand. It's not the *chosen* anything. It's when you are ready for things that they will happen. Why should a person stay in kindergarten forever, to wait for everybody else? They may never progress.

The shaman told me I was given *carte blanche* because I have a heart, because I care. I truly care. I don't want to see any more suffering. I don't want to see people hurting people. I hate treachery. I hate all of that! I want to live in a place where I can walk out on the street and say hello and not have somebody jeer at me, as though they are thinking, "Gee, what is that person saying hello and smiling for? What does she want?" Being a female, if you smile at a guy, they think, "Ah-ha. She's ready." Well, I want to live in a world for our children and grandchildren's sake, in a world of freedom. If you want to sit and do nothing, it's your choice.

Frank said he would see me again. I hope so. So far just about everything he has told me has come to pass. The predictions he made involved the shifting of our planet's axis. He said there are now some aliens working very hard from certain planets, trying to help keep this earth from tilting. That's why we have all these hurricanes and things that are happening right now. I know of a man who is a healer, whose name I will keep anonymous, who knows of another planet. He knows the various space people who come here and he verified and has shown me that they have been working very hard on this for almost a year now—without much success— but they're trying.

Unfortunately, a lot of things are going to happen even more, which I know myself. You have to understand we are polluting this planet. Logically speaking, if the air isn't good to breathe, how long do you think humankind will last? If we are wreaking so much havoc to our environment, look at the illness which this will bring. People become mutated. We have no place even for our garbage. Nobody has come up with any answers. Scientists were told a while ago about the greenhouse effect and they have shrugged it off. Now they are sitting in Geneva, saying that they cannot go back to help where it was, because now it is too late. And if the ice melts from the northern pole, then water will flood our cities and everywhere.

I think that is what upstairs actually meant. They tried to disarm all of the nuclear weapons, and yet—it's funny—people seem to want the Americans to arm themselves again because they feel the Russians are not disarming. I really don't know what is going on. Wherever I turn, I see disaster. That's the only thing that scares me. That's why I am working as hard as I am.

For the ordinary people of this planet, this is their last Earth incarnation. If Earth people are able to raise their spiritual level, or conscious level, just one little interval, they will have a better life in the next lifetime. If they do not, they will really be lost. As my contact said, "There will be many who will go to sleep for eons of years, and until they find another habitable planet, they will be placed back on Earth, where they will have to start all over again."

Just think about it. All the eons of lifetimes that have made you and me—all that we had to go through—they will have to go through that again, right from the beginning. That's why I am working so hard, to help the ordinary individual evolve, to try to get rid of all the various problems that bog them down to the materialistic gods they have enshrined. When they cheat and lie and do everything they shouldn't, they don't know themselves.

And that's why I am working so hard.

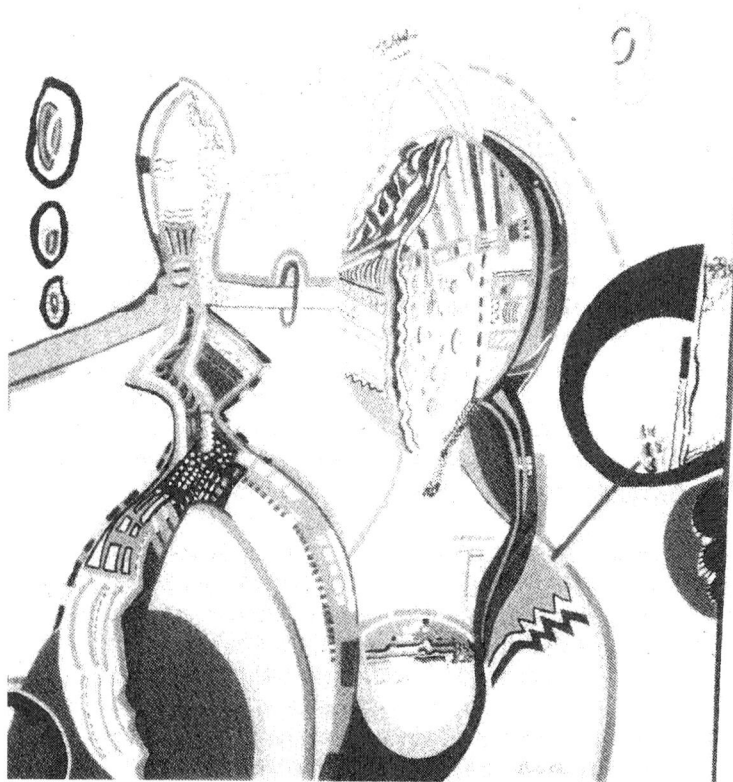

Chapter 9

Hypnotic Regression

October 18, 1988 with Ellie Arnold

The following is the transcript from my regression session with Ellie Arnold in British Columbia. Peter Arnold, Ellie's husband, sat in on this session. They were both born in Holland and emigrated to Canada in 1957 with their three small children. Ellie is a regressionist. She does regression therapy on past lives, memories, and works to release the negative to the positive. She studied in both Canada and the United States. She volunteers for a local crisis center.

EA: We're now going to work a little with the higher conscious. And we're asking the higher conscious. And we're asking the higher conscious if you would like to go back in time. We'd like to go back to your first contact with the space people in this lifetime. We would like to go back in this life to maybe approximately 1958. We'd like to go back to your first contact with the space people in this life. We are now asking the higher conscious, what floor should you go to? In order to get that memory back, in order to perceive that and to relive that, we are now asking the higher conscious what floor should you go to? We trust again whatever number comes in.

SKC: Eight.

EA: The eighth floor. Good. We now will do the normal thing. I'm going to ask you to push the button for the doors. When the doors are closed, I would like you to push the button for the eighth floor. When the elevator goes up, I would like you to count out the floors aloud for me while you are passing them.

SKC: One ...

EA: Good.

SKC: Two ...

EA: Mm-hm.

SKC: Three ...

EA: Good.

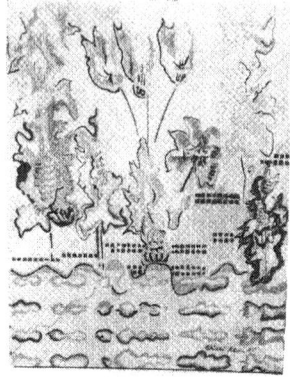

In the Blue Planet — the flowers were mostly blue — an array of the most beautiful colours I ever saw.

SKC: Four ... five ...

EA: Mm-hm.

SKC: Six ...

EA: Good.

SKC: Seven ... eight ...

EA: You have now arrived at the right floor for you. At the outside of the elevator there's the beginning of that memory that has opened up, and the first scene that you will find outside the elevator for you. It will be a nice clear scene for you. To begin with, let's have a look at the doors of the elevator and find out if they're open or closed. What can you tell me?

SKC: They're open.

EA: Great. Great. I'm going to ask you to take a step forward out of the elevator, and let me know when you've done that.

SKC: I've stepped out ...

EA: Okay, now take another step forward. Let me know when you've done that.

SKC: I've stepped forward.

EA: Now I would like you to have a good look around you and see and sense where you are at that particular time. Where do you find yourself at this time? Are you indoors or outdoors?

SKC: I'm in some sort of crystal or mirror ... I don't know.

EA: Okay, let's have a look at the ground ... are you sitting or standing?

SKC: I am standing.

EA: You are standing. Can you tell me ...

SKC: It's moving. I'm moving with it.

EA: You are moving with it. All right. Where are you moving from?

SKC: All I see is crystal ... like a crystal dome.

EA: Are you moving towards the crystal dome?

SKC: I seem to be in it.

EA: You seem to be in the crystal dome.

SKC: In this crystal dome ... it's like squares, all square all around.

EA: Okay, can you have a look at yourself? What are you dressed in at that particular time? What are you wearing?

SKC: I'm wearing something strange.

EA: How strange? How does it look to you?

SKC: Like a sort of a jump suit.

EA: Are you by yourself, or are there other people around you?

SKC: I'm by myself this very moment.

EA: You're by yourself at this very moment. All right, let's arrive at your destination, because you seem to be going someplace. Let's move forward just a little in time until you have arrived at your destination. We do that very easily. We use two little words for that ... right now. When I say right now, you will have arrived at wherever you are going.

SKC: The door is opening.

EA: Good.

SKC: Of this dome. I'm stepping out. I see a lot of people. They're all dressed like I am dressed. They're coming to greet me. They're taking me somewhere.

EA: All right.

SKC: Where are they taking me? There's a strange vehicle. I'm stepping in that vehicle. I have a person inside with me. We're driving. We stop. We're going up some strange steps. There seems to be somebody sitting on some strange ... it's not a throne exactly. Sort of a small podium.

EA: Is that inside that vehicle?

SKC: No, outside. I stepped out of the vehicle and walked up some stairs. That person knows me, and he has a strange greeting. His hand is out, and turning the schist or a strange salute. [*A hand was placed over his heart with two fingers protruding.*] I seem to know this person.

EA: Does this person communicate with you other than the salute?

SKC: He wants me to come closer. He's taking me around, and that greeting ... I seem to be known, for some reason or another.

EA: Is there some verbal communication going on there?

SKC: No.

EA: Is there any other means of communication going on there?

SKC: No, it seems to be all telepathic.

EA: So that's the means of communication, so you communicate telepathically. All right, are you seeing people? Do they appear like what we consider Earth people, or do they appear differently to you?

SKC: No, they appear the same as we do.

EA: Okay.

SKC: There doesn't seem to be anything that they look different. They're handsome people. They're more of the blondish type of people. The females are very, very, very beautiful. So are the males. They're just beautiful people. They seem to be going about doing their things. This man that has greeted me seems to know me very well. Oh, just a second, there's somebody else coming into the room who also seems very happy to see me. They're husband and wife, I think, or they're man and woman.

EA: Okay. Yes?

SKC: They're talking amongst themselves. The greeting that they're giving me or telling me is that they're happy to see me.

EA: Okay.

SKC: But they want me to leave. I have to go back. They've summoned somebody to take me back.

EA: Take you back where?

SKC: Take me back on this vehicle. It's on tracks, and I'm saying my goodbyes, and I'm leaving. I'm going back with ... they have something for me, but they've decided not to give it to me.

EA: Okay. Are they communicating to you that they have something for you?

SKC: Yes. I don't know ... I ... I saw a glimpse of it. It's some sort of crystal ball or something. They decided not to give it to me. I'm going back down the stairs, back into the vehicle, with the same messenger or whatever it is that took me. He's bringing me back. They also have a sort of strange salute, but putting his hand on his chest and waving it. And that's sort of a goodbye. Stepping back into that crystal ... I don't know if it's a dome or what. I don't know.

EA: Could it be considered a crystal sphere?

SKC: Possibly. I'm going back. I'm in it. It's moving again. I'm still on it. I really don't know where I'm going, but I think I'm not frightened.

EA: Good.

SKC: I'm ending up in the house where I used to live in Montreal. I find myself back in the bed, on the opposite direction of the bed. There's these two space people looking at me and finding out whether they should take me. And as I'm looking at them, they're ... and they disappear. I guess that's it.

EA: Okay, let's now contact the higher conscious for a few seconds. And ask the higher conscious to release the information from the subconscious. In our concept of calendar years, what is the year at that particular time?

SKC: 1962.

EA: Okay, okay. In our concept of, let's say space and/or geography, where did they take you? Where did you ...

SKC: To Noosus ... Noosus ... I don't even know where Noosus is.

EA: All right. Then, we're asking the higher conscious to be aware and to tune into where Noosus is on our, let's say galactic map, so that when you are in your normal state of awareness, you will be able to find it on the map of the galaxies. Let's now slowly move this scene behind. And we're moving forward a little in time and space, and we're moving forward to the next important experience that you had with the space contact. We're moving forward in this life to your next contact with the space people ... easily ... we're moving forward, leaving the scene behind us ... to your next contact, time and place, and we arrive there and easily right now. Let's see where we find you now and what is happening at this particular time. Where are you now?

SKC: I'm in the shop on Fourth Avenue with my contact.

EA: You are seeing your contact. How do you know this is contact?

SKC: I have seen him many, many times. He is a contact.

EA: Has he told you he is a contact?

SKC: Yes, he is an alien from a planet. He said it was very far away, not in this galaxy, and many galaxies away.

EA: All right, so this particular time you're meeting the contact. What is happening?

SKC: Well, this was a physical contact. I would only go to the shop to get information, and he would tell me many things, and I even introduced him to some of my friends. He was just a very loving person.

EA: Did he give you the information that you came for?

SKC: Little by little, yes he did. A lot of things I asked for, he said I wasn't ready to ... to receive them, because I wouldn't understand it. So he said he had to be careful because I had a way of worming things out of him. He would get hell for it, for telling me, so I knew I had to stop.

EA: This contact ... how long has he been on Earth?

SKC: He's been on Earth ... uh, well this lifetime, actually ... he was in Saskatchewan. He had to help one of his ... he's like an agent and he was assigning, like sub-agents which ... I'm one of his sub-agents, working for my agent. He had to help the various sub-agents reach a level of consciousness and to try to rid a lot of the karma that was attached to the sub-agents.

EA: So this contact was also born on Earth?

SKC: I don't think so. He loaned a body.

EA: Okay. Let's again leave this scene behind us, and move forward to your next meeting or contact with those that are important to you. Move forward again to your next ... see where we find you now.

SKC: You find me saying goodbye to my ... my friend, where he hands me eight [copper] plates and he told me that they were my driver's license, and my medical, and all the things pertaining when I leave this planet. I don't think so, but that's what he told me.

EA: That's what he told you. Okay, what's the size of these [copper] plates?

SKC: I think they're five inches by four inches.

EA: All right, let's contact the higher conscious. Let's ask the higher conscious who can tune into all memory. Let's ask the higher conscious what the purpose is of these [copper] plates, and trust whatever flows in.

SKC: I think they were given to me so that when I tell people about my experiences they would believe me. I also think that since they would probably be used in a spacecraft, because they have the binary code, but a different kind of binary code, and some of the plates, I think, are my … that other space people will know that I have them, so when the time comes they will be in contact with me, because I have been found worthy of these plates. I was told that there are eight other people in the world that have these plates. But what are on them? In a language totally unknown to me.

EA: Okay, you haven't been able to decipher what is on them.

SKC: No, I do know one of them has my voice chartered, that if and when I will run a spacecraft that my voice will activate the spacecraft. That one I'm really sure of. But the meaning of the others, I don't know. I think it's just for the other aliens to know that I have them and there's messages on them for them. I never thought of that … that's interesting.

EA: Let's again slowly leave this scene behind, and again move through memory to the next important encounter with the space people. Slowly move forward again to the next important encounter with the space people. And again we arrive there, easily and comfortably and … right now. Right now. Let's see where you find yourself now.

SKC: I find myself somewhere unknown.

EA: All right. Can you describe it at all to me?

SKC: Yah, there are blue trees. The grass is blue. Animals are around, but I think they are very quiet animals. There's a white horse ... seems to be a pale blue sky. There's flowers, all different color flowers ... there's somebody running up towards me.

EA: Okay, describe the person or entity that is running up towards you.

SKC: She's a lady with long hair. She's wearing an apron, I don't know why, and she's taking both my hands and asking me to come with her. I'm going with her, and we're going on sort of a sidewalk that moves. And we're on this sidewalk. We're moving. And not very far there's a strange-looking house on stilts, and the sidewalk is stopped, but it's a sort of a ... it raises up towards the door. We're going in there, and the smells are so nice. Warm, friendly ... and she's offering me something to eat. It's a very tiny little house, just enough for one person. Nice pictures on the wall ... I'm sitting there, and she's busying herself all around, and as I said, she offered me something. I have refused it. I don't what it is. I don't know whether to take it.

EA: Ask the higher conscious what is your purpose of being there.

SKC: It was one of my lifetimes ... past lifetimes. I was there.

EA: Okay, so let's ask the higher conscious different questions. At this particular time are you tuning into a past lifetime, or is it a memory from a past lifetime that is coming up?

SKC: A memory of a past lifetime.

EA: Okay, let's ask the higher conscious to release the information from the subconscious. The place that you're at, at that particular time, in our concept of geography, is it on Earth or is it outside of Earth?

SKC: It's outside of Earth.

EA: Okay. Can we ask what the name of the planet or star is that you're on?

SKC: I don't know where it comes from. It's … Plexy.

EA: All right.

SKC: Plexy.

EA: Did you live there?

SKC: Yes, I lived there.

EA: What kind of a life did you have there? What was your main purpose in that life?

SKC: I was sort of looking after animals … kind of a shepherd. Very quiet, just like this lady here. I think probably that was me.

EA: Okay.

SKC: I didn't have a very exciting life. I seem to have lived there by myself. As I look around the room, I don't see any pictures of any men or family or anything.

EA: No, not every lifetime is very exciting.

SKC: I seem to be living completely alone. Maybe I had to …

contemplation. I don't know.

EA: Let's ask the higher conscious to give us the most important experience in that lifetime. Ask the higher conscious to release ...

SKC: Talking to the animals ... by communication with animals, and if I recollect, my contact told me that I had to know how to talk to animals. Ah-ha, that's interesting. So I used to talk to the animals. I should be able to do it again. Isn't that interesting? I didn't know that. I had forgotten that. That's why I was there, that's why all the animals ... I see, ah-hah. That's very interesting.

EA: Let's very slowly again leave this place behind us, and move a little through time and space. Let's ask the higher conscious to again bring us to an episode in this life. You've had some input in your ... and you phrased it ... you had an implant. We would like to slowly move to the first time, to the very first implant that was put in.

SKC: I was around five years old when it was put down, given to me. I was in the bedroom where I heard a noise. I went out. I took a blanket with me. I almost tripped down the stairs because there was a staircase there. There was a person there I have never seen before, yet I wasn't frightened of that person.

EA: Okay.

SKC: He touched the back of my neck. He told me not to worry. Everything will be all right. And he just disappeared. I walked up those stairs, carrying a blanket ... to go back in my little room and to bed ... and that's all I remember of that.

EA: Okay, and did you remember the next morning what happened?

SKC: No.

EA: No. All right, so you also told me before we started that you had another implant.

SKC: Yes.

EA: So what we'd like to do now is to slowly again ... right now. Right now.

SKC: I was asleep. My body was asleep, but I wasn't there.

EA: How old are you now?

SKC: How old am I now?

EA: How old are you when that happened?

SKC: This happened a few ... I'd say about a year ago.

EA: Okay, and you're saying your body is asleep.

SKC: My body's asleep. I wasn't there.

EA: Okay, where were you?

SKC: I was on a slab. I was being checked again ... my body. A needle was put on me when I was so angry, I jumped out of that slab ... I guess, got into my body, because I jumped out of bed because I was angry that they did that to me without asking me. They didn't ask me the first time, and now again ... and now I'm asking. Why?

EA: Okay.

SKC: I have things I have to do. They're awakening my
subconscious. I have things that I have to do, and that it's
time to do them now.

EA: So let's ask the higher conscious what is it that you are
supposed to do now ... the time is now, you are saying.
What is it that it is time for now?

SKC: It's time to reveal everything that I know.

EA: How long do you think that took to put the implant in? Our
concept of time ...

SKC: Moments ... a moment.

EA: All right, all right. And when you arrived back in your body,
did you remember what had happened?

SKC: Only that I was on a ship, on a slab, and how I got there I
don't know. I guess I just got there.

EA: All right, let's move back a little to just before it happened.
Let's move back a little, just before it happened. And
again we arrive that easily and comfortably ... right now.

SKC: Two people came on my side to tell me that it was time for
me to go with them. I went. We flew up to the spacecraft
... we're hovering ...

EA: Okay, and then you say we flew up. How did that occur?

SKC: They both took my hand and we elevated [*floated, slowly
lifted up*]. And we went right in. I was put on the slab,
where they checked me with various instruments about

my body and what was happening.

EA: The people that worked with you ... did they ... do they look like what we would consider Earth people on Earth to look?

SKC: I think these two people that took me up were kind of like a human robot. I didn't see their faces, but felt them, and their hands. I felt their hands. Their hands were flesh because they were holding me, but I didn't see their faces. On the slab they looked through to see how I was doing, and when they started to put that needle in ... as I said ... how I ended up in my body and jumping out of bed is something I don't really know how that happened.

EA: Okay. Now the people that were probing you in the spacecraft, did they also look like robots?

SKC: No, the one that was checking my body was not. He didn't talk to me, but he just ... he took an instrument and checked me. I allowed that, but only when they stuck that needle in ... I wasn't very happy about that, because all they can do is tell me what I should do and I'll do it, if it's within the good of humanity. But they didn't do that. All they did was stick that needle in, and I am still angry.

EA: They say that's a very natural reaction. I think personally I would be angry too. Did they realize that you were angry?

SKC: Yah. I was told recently not to be angry because this will awaken various things that they wanted me ... that I will be able to do.

EA: You are saying the people that probed you looked similar, like people on Earth?

SKC: I think so. I didn't really look that closely because I had my eyes sort of closed a little bit.

EA: Okay. So again, let's slowly and comfortably ... we're going to work a little longer with the higher conscious. We're going to ask the higher conscious if you've had several encounters with space people. Now asking the higher conscious where all these encounters ... these space people that were associated with the encounters ... were they all the same people, or did they come from different areas from outer space?

SKC: No. I'm afraid it was from the same group. It seems that I was told that I've done ... the work that I'm doing now I have done before. Now they have need of me. They have need of my personality. I seem to be able to draw people to me. And because of my honesty, they require that at this time.

EA: Let's ask the higher conscious what was the purpose of the implants?

SKC: The implants is ... that they can send me messages. I would be able to pick up a lot of what my next step is, and it also is a protective ... to tell me that people were going to harm me, to keep away ...

EA: Let's ask the higher conscious what was the purpose of the probing?

SKC: The probing of where?

EA: With the needle.

SKC: Again, I require this also for protective measures. They're in contact with me at all times.

EA: Let's ask the higher conscious, were there any additional or any more contacts that you have forgotten about, or that you have sort of put away in the subconscious, that on a conscious level you do not remember? Address a yes or a no on that.

SKC: I say, no.

EA: Okay. Slowly and easily we go to a very nice, comfortable place. We float a little through time and space. It's comfortable, it's peaceful, and you're going to a lovely meadow. It's a beautiful day there. You can see wildflowers growing in the meadow. You can see in the distance there's a little bit of a river in the landscape. There's a beautiful waterfall splashing in the river. You're going to sit down close to the waterfall. Such a peaceful place, a very spiritual place, a meeting place. And we're going to make ourselves really comfortable there. We're going to work at this particular time ... we're going to work with the higher conscious, and we're going to ask the higher conscious a few questions. We're going to begin with asking from now on, from this day in your present life, is your life going to change? And we trust a yes or a no on that. Is your life going to ...

SKC: Yes.

EA: Okay, can we ask the higher conscious how is it going to change? What are the changes that are going to occur?

SKC: I'm going to have spiritual experiences, more awareness, and I'll be helping more and more people. I'll be meeting more people.

EA: The place where we're in right now is also a very spiritual place. It's a place where we meet guides. It's a place where we can meet those that have passed over, who are asking higher conscious at this time. We would like to meet some of your guides. We're asking the higher conscious if it is possible for them to come and appear on the meadow and be in contact with you. And we trust a yes or a no on that. Is it possible for your guides to come out and be in contact with you on the meadow?

SKC: Yes.

EA: Good. Then again, this works very nice and easy, when the guides decide to come out, they let you know by a yes, we are available, and in the distance we can see them appearing. It may be one, it may be more than ...

SKC: Oh, I've got so many.

EA: Isn't that nice.

SKC: One ... two ... three ... four ... five ... six ... seven ... eight ... nine ... ten ... eleven ... I have eleven guides.

EA: Isn't that lovely. At this particular time I'm going to switch the tape over. It's going to make a little clicking ... it will only relax you more.

END OF TAPE SIDE ONE
SIDE TWO:

EA: ... would be the spokes energy or spokesperson for them, and to begin with, we say hello to them. And we send them all our love, and we ask these particular energy what his or her name is.

SKC: His name is Yok ... Yok ...

EA: Can you ask him, does he have a message for you?

SKC: He's smiling. He says, I don't need any messages. I know. I know.

EA: Okay. Is there anything you want to ask them?

SKC: No.

EA: All right.

SKC: I thank them.

EA: Great.

SKC: I know we are in communication because when I require any assistance, I first call them. It was given to me.

EA: Now ask the guides and your higher conscious, we would like to contact your mother. We're asking if that is possible.

SKC: No, it's not, not yet.

EA: Okay. Can we contact your father?

SKC: No, he's with my mother.

EA: All right, so what we do at this particular time is just send our love and you know that it will be received.

SKC: Yes, I think so …

EA: Now, while you're in that nice, beautiful, peaceful meadow there, with your guides around you, is there anything else that you want to find out?

SKC: No, I don't think so.

EA: Anything that you want to ask?

SKC: No.

EA: Okay.

SKC: I know I'm being protected. I know I'm being led in the right direction.

EA: All right. So slowly and comfortably you're coming back to today. We do that with a three count. At the end of the three count you'll be fully aware on all levels again. It's a totally normal feeling, just great, to be mentally alert again, remembering everything and working so positive with it, and that you are already doing … and spiritually and emotionally, completely serene … and in tune and in harmony with the universe. So slowly I'm going to count up to one, two, three, and at the end of the three count you'll be fully aware on all levels again. Fully aware on all levels again, remembing everything, working so positive with it. Realizing that you can do anything you want, and accomplishing anything that you want. And spiritually and emotionally serene. One … you can feel that nice life energy flowing through the whole of your body … it's healthy, totally great. Two … mentally alert again, mentally alert again, remembering everything, working so positive with it. At this particular time I would like you to rub your two fingers together. And at the count of three you will be fully aware on all levels and spiritually and emotionally serene. Three! Back to today. And you can open your eyes and move your legs a little and take your time to balance all. Stretch a little.

END OF REGRESSION

My reaction to this regression session:

It flowed. Everything came out. I was relaxed. I don't think I was completely under. Things came. I saw pictures actually. That's how I described things. But remember, too, that I am an artist and I see things in pictures, so I don't know if that's a general reaction or because it's me. It came easily. I had a good feeling. When I arrived at the session, I was uptight, but not when I left. Ellie made me feel comfortable.

I sort of felt that I have been in space many times, and my contact had told me I had been in space for most of my incarnations, so I wasn't shocked by what took place in the regression. It's not always easy for us to remember. It was there for me and I simply described what I saw. I don't believe I can make up things like that. I try to be as honest as I can.

Chapter 10

Contact from Sirius-B

In May 1983, during a visit to Paris, I attended a séance with my friend, David MacKenzie-Thornton. David is a spiritualist who has ongoing communications with people from the beyond. He is told so many things and knows many famous names. He was introduced to space through me. Somehow George Major, an etheric being from Sirius-B, came through one day. The medium at this séance was Allan McDougall. In this transcript, dated May 12, 1983, David MacKenzie-Thornton used a stereo tape recorder to later interpret the dialogue. The entity Peter came through first.

Date: May 12, 1983   Location: Paris

PETER: Not all persons in physical bodies naturally belong to the earth plane. They are utilizing physical bodies because they're expected to have a body of that type on the earth plane.

DAVID: Where do they get the bodies from?

PETER: It's a natural body, often loaned for that purpose. But in some cases borrowed ... or bought ... or traded.

SHIRLÈ: Is that a walk-in?

PETER: No, a walk-in is done without permission. What I'm speaking of is an exchange. The rightful owner may often be given another situation.

SHIRLÈ: He said he was coming back for me.

PETER: He may well take another body, but it may well be one of his colleagues.

SHIRLÈ: He told me I am very important, and I don't know yet what my direction should be.

PETER: I am not able to advise at that level.

DAVID: Are these people so much more advanced than we are, wherever they come from?

PETER: Perhaps intellectually, yes. [*He speaks of reincarnation … between the earth plane and other planes of existence on the planet.*]

DAVID: Are they incarnated on a physical or an etheric planet?

PETER: Etheric. [*He goes on to suggest that some of these people we are talking about may be in a physical body on a physical planet, but it is unusual.*] Etheric bodies.

DAVID: Something like George Major, with whom we've had a visit?

PETER: Yes, Sirius-B.

DAVID: That is where George Major comes from—an etheric planet?

PETER: [*There's some confusion here because he says Sirius-B was and still is a physical planet, he believes.*]

SHIRLÈ: I was told I was going to leave here physically to go to another planet.

PETER: I do not know about that, but it could be possible.

SHIRLÈ: I was told I was from another planet. Was I?

PETER: I think not, but I will not be the final judge on this matter. It's a complex subject, especially with the mix of souls and personalities, and it is perhaps possible that a part of a person could be from another planet.

DAVID: It becomes very complex indeed.

SHIRLÈ: I think it is quite easy.

PETER: Perhaps Shirlè is intellectually allied to the inter-planetary idea.

SHIRLÈ: Yes, that is what Frank told me.

PETER: It's quite complicated and I've had little dealings with it.

DAVID: Do you know anybody who has had dealings with it, because it's very important to Shirlè. Is there anybody there who could talk a little bit about it?

PETER: I'll send a call.

Here there is a pause. David says, "In my version I summarize quite a lot and I don't necessarily use the same words as in the original (version). This is particularly true of George Major, since he has troubles in translation and hesitates a lot, especially in the first part of his talk."

[Enter George Major.]

GEORGE MAJOR: Good evening.

DAVID: George Major, hello, George. Have you come to talk to us about your planet and our friend's mission here?

GEORGE MAJOR: I have spoken of our concern for your planet. We have tried many times to protect you from exterior action without actually entering into the politics of your countries. Only from the outside. It has not been altogether successful.

DAVID: No, it would seem not.

GEORGE MAJOR: We have for several of your Earth years taken an intenser interest. We could not do this in our own form. On this first point we are not physical bodies. We are at the etheric level. It is necessary for us to acquire a physical form to interact with your world. We will not forcibly eject the owner from his rightful place. We have at times found the persons who will give us the use of their bodies. Sometimes on a permanent basis, sometimes leasehold. In that way we are able to interact with your world, but there are others who are not so honest in their campaign. They tend to steal the bodies.

DAVID: Are these people from other etheric planets?

GEORGE MAJOR: Yes.

DAVID: It's a kind of war then.

GEORGE MAJOR: [He agrees.]

DAVID: What about Frank? Was he from Sirius-B?

GEORGE MAJOR: Yes, he was from Sirius-B.

DAVID: Did you know of him?

GEORGE MAJOR: I did not know him personally, but I knew of his mission.

DAVID: What was that? Was it to prepare certain people for departure?

GEORGE MAJOR: It was to help in the re-education of the nations of the world. [*He's having trouble in translation here because first he says 'in training' for departure, and he ends up saying 're-education of the nations of the world'.*]

DAVID: Why would it be necessary for Shirlè to leave her planet aboard one of your spaceships?

GEORGE MAJOR: I think there has been a misunderstanding. Earth people are unlikely to visit Sirius-B in their physical bodies. They can do so in their astral form. The spaceships are not physical spacecraft themselves.

DAVID: Yes, physical people cannot go aboard a non-physical spacecraft. I suggest if you are in the astral body you travel anyway.

GEORGE MAJOR: But there is danger in interplanetary travel, which leaves the astral body unprotected. It is energy in itself and so can be affected by other energies.

DAVID: Is this by physical energies?

GEORGE MAJOR: Yes, but I am speaking more about electromagnetic energies from the planets and the great suns. So, we make a spacecraft of an etheric nature to act as a protective shield. There are many Earth persons who have traveled in these spacecraft. I would hesitate to say they have hallucinated, but they have seen their own ideas of a physical spacecraft.

DAVID: They have traveled in them?

GEORGE MAJOR: Oh yes, they have traveled in them. Many of your Earth persons have already visited the various planets.

DAVID: Etheric planets?

GEORGE MAJOR: Yes.

DAVID: Why wouldn't they land?

GEORGE MAJOR: Because of the consequences. A planet of the nature of Venus would not be suitable for an Earth person, even in the astral body. It would perhaps be harmful.

DAVID: But what about Sirius-B?

GEORGE MAJOR: As I have mentioned on a previous occasion, our residents live in the great sea. They would have to be taken on a spacecraft under the sea. And then they could emerge and so could we, under the protection of the sea, and visit our training colleges. Our problem is with radiation from Sirius.

DAVID: Yes, to protect yourselves on your etheric planet with your etheric people, protect yourselves from the physical radiation on Sirius-B, you live under the great sea.

GEORGE MAJOR: I think you misunderstand a little about radiation. There is radiation of an atomic nature, which you would call radioactive. And there is radiation of an electromagnetic nature ... heat, light ... a system of electromagnetic waves which are not altogether physical. They're on the border between the two. For that reason you are able to communicate with the spirit world, because of the electromagnetic magnetism. Radio communication, for example. This is the electromagnetic radiation, which is very intense, which causes us the problems.

DAVID: Particularly from Sirius? The sun Sirius? Are you using the word 'planets' to describe all of this in space?

GEORGE MAJOR: I'm thinking particularly of planets in the scientific sense. One would not conceive of visiting a sun.

DAVID: No, we certainly couldn't anyway. And Sirius is a sun, a star, a sun.

GEORGE MAJOR: Yes.

DAVID: Well, Sirius-B being etheric, you are still much concerned with this radiation, and is that what made Sirius-C disappear?

GEORGE MAJOR: It was one of these planets, which was in its physical state, experimenting with subnuclear forces. The state of your world is dangerously hot with your nuclear weapons, but they went the next step—the energy which controls these forces—and they disintegrated their planet.

DAVID: There's nothing left?

GEORGE MAJOR: But there are still some of them around. Yes, they did not destroy the souls. They destroyed the physical and the etheric.

DAVID: You don't want that to happen, do you?

GEORGE MAJOR: Certainly not. We do not wish a physical destruction of your world.

DAVID: Physical destruction of the planet Earth would seriously affect you?

GEORGE MAJOR: Oh yes, and all the planets in the solar system. And that would not be good for us. We're not being selfish. We do not want to see the destruction of any physical existence on any planet. We would not wish to see needless extinction, be it physical, etheric or astral.

DAVID: What do you consider to be the difference between etheric and astral?

GEORGE MAJOR: It's a question of solidity … of solidarity. The astral form is of an electromagnetic structure. The etheric form has electromagnetic structure but is also supplied with a large quantity of particles of a subphysical nature. You will find that it is indeed quite solid.

DAVID: I suppose it depends on who's looking at it, but to them it is quite solid.

GEORGE MAJOR: Yes. The physical realm is very dense, very solid. And the etheric is a thousand times less solid than that. And the astral perhaps a thousand times less solid again.

DAVID: But you as etheric beings have your astral bodies, too?

GEORGE MAJOR: Oh yes.

DAVID: Frank was using the astral body to borrow one of our bodies?

GEORGE MAJOR: That is so.

SHIRLÈ: Why was I chosen to help?

GEORGE MAJOR: You had the right psychological make-up and were approachable. Not everybody is approachable. Many of our agents are simply rejected, but not so many. But many persons would reject their proposals. However, our agents are trained to select people. They are trained to select the correct persons. I was trying to make a point. It is not in every person in our world who would accept such a proposal ... to act as an assistant to their agent.

DAVID: So what is the help to be? What help is Shirlè to give?

GEORGE MAJOR: I don't have the details on this particular project. I think it is to make people aware of the intelligences around, that they can be contacted if one desires to do so. And at the proper stage, practical help will be given, if it is asked for. If one or two persons cannot give help for the entire world, there must be at least a consensus of opinion. Many more persons will be needed.

DAVID: Are we seeing something like that already with all the protest demonstrations against nuclear war?

GEORGE MAJOR: Yes, this was one of our early projects. We implanted ideas and this was somewhat frowned upon by what one might call our ethical standards committee. There was not sufficient consultation before the project was put under way. We were accused of interfering with the minds of the people in whom the ideas had been implanted. But also not working out the long-term consequences. And many persons were injured. We hope to put forward a peace campaign that will be beneficial and unharmful to people.

DAVID: That kind of peace campaign can be mounted in our country, in America, in England, in France, in West Germany. But if you try to do that in Russia, a lot of people are going to be hurt.

GEORGE MAJOR: Yes, that is one of the problems. It was the same thing in Russia, but it was quickly squashed. We now have a new project, and it's making good progress, although it is unlikely that you will hear much about it for some while through official channels. In that way, if the majority of people in any country desire something, the government has to eventually oblige.

SHIRLÈ: What about my eight engraved copper plates? I want to know what the correct answer is.

GEORGE MAJOR: I do not know anything about these particular plates.

SHIRLÈ: Frank gave me eight plates … copper plates … with writing on them. [*She explains that a lady friend told her the writing was Atlantis writing.*]

GEORGE MAJOR: The lady was saying that it was Atlantis writing?

SHIRLÈ: Yes.

GEORGE MAJOR: It is quite possible that decipherers date from this time. They had disc plates for communication purposes.

SHIRLÈ: But the plates are square, not round.

GEORGE MAJOR: Maybe these are different. Frank's are different. There are similar patterns for making communications.

DAVID: Are they physical metal like ours?

GEORGE MAJOR: Certainly. I am talking about normal persons in your physical world. The agent [*the person working for them*] is given this communications medium. They can use it to make a telepathic communication with their leader and also with several of their local agents.

SHIRLÈ: Are they very important?

GEORGE MAJOR: Certainly. Don't throw them away.

SHIRLÈ: Oh no, I have them in the bank. He told me that's where I should put them, and I did.

GEORGE MAJOR: It's better to leave them in the bank for the moment. You're not ready to use them yet and you will be given instruction on how to use them.

DAVID: What about the Atlantis writing on the plates?

GEORGE MAJOR: I'd say they were from the Atlantic period.

DAVID: When was that? Because it is legend to us.

GEORGE MAJOR: The writing is the same as that which is Atlantis, but because the writing is the same it doesn't mean it's Atlantean writing, which would infer the discs themselves were from Atlantis. Shirlè's discs, or discs like Shirlè's, are fabricated on Earth by their technicians under a special process. They use that process of writing because it is of a special geometric form which has a power in itself. The Atlanteans knew this and used it in many of their temples.

DAVID: Are you inferring that Atlantis did exist?

GEORGE MAJOR: Yes, indeed it did. It was not, of course, called Atlantis, but it was indeed a highly advanced civilization. The Atlanteans came close to using the subnuclear forces. They eventually destroyed their own civilization, but the planet remained intact.

DAVID: How many years ago was this, in our language?

GEORGE MAJOR: I'm talking about five or six thousand years ago. It's difficult to place. Atlanteans had the power, but luckily they didn't go very far with it. They only blew up their continent.

DAVID: Was this in what we call the Atlantic?

GEORGE MAJOR: It's a place in America … in a place where North America joins South America. It used to be almost as wide all the way down. It also extended somewhat further south in the middle of what we call America— the tail going south. And there are some remains in the shape of little islands in the ocean … the part which didn't entirely get destroyed.

DAVID: Is this the Caribbean?

GEORGE MAJOR: Yes, it was.

DAVID: Are we close to that point?

GEORGE MAJOR: Oh, you've got a few good years to go yet.

DAVID: Do you have an accelerated program now which is beginning to produce good results?

GEORGE MAJOR: There are acceptable phenomena … a good start. Some people will start listening. And I do think we will have a very good chance of saving the planet. We can show you better ways of living than being aggressive all the time.

DAVID: I certainly hope you can.

SHIRLÈ: I'm trying to do everything I can.

GEORGE MAJOR: It's not easy, but it's better than total annihilation. It's not altogether that gloomy. Your world is not going to blow itself up tomorrow, we think. But we have to take a long-term view and we look centuries ahead, making provision now, not hundreds of years in the future.

DAVID: How old are you?

GEORGE MAJOR: I'm a young man … about 1,500.

SHIRLÈ: I would like confirmation that somebody else will come back to me in six months' time.

GEORGE MAJOR: Frank may be able to reincarnate and come back, but I believe it's more likely that another will come.

SHIRLÈ: Peter said he thought it would be in six months.

GEORGE MAJOR: It takes a little while to make arrangements, but I hope that that will be the case—that somebody will come in six months' time and will contact you.

DAVID: George, have you been able to talk to any other people like Shirlè?

GEORGE MAJOR: I have one … in Montreal, I think.

DAVID: Do you know his or her name?

GEORGE MAJOR: It's a little gentleman … Markin, I think, Markin, Ralph Markin. [*We have trouble sorting out the spelling, Markin or Marken. But it seems it's Ralph Markin.*]

SHIRLÈ: I can look in the phone book.

GEORGE MAJOR: It's close to a market … an old market.

SHIRLÈ: That's the old city of Montreal.

GEORGE MAJOR: [*It may be Market Street, Mr. Markin of Market Street.*] I'm not entirely certain about this. It's not very often that we have to say the names.

DAVID: Well, if you cannot find it today, perhaps you will let us know later, or let Shirlè know.

GEORGE MAJOR: I'm not very good at writing these days.

SHIRLÈ: I will stop in Montreal and try to find him.

DAVID: Do you think that will be worthwhile if she contacts him?

GEORGE MAJOR: Yes, it will be worth a trial. He's a medium and not an assistant agent. Ralph Markin is a medium, not an assistant agent like Shirlè.

DAVID: George, you've been able to clear up some misunderstandings tonight on this subject.

SHIRLÈ: You've been wonderful and I appreciate it.

GEORGE MAJOR: It's an interesting project, the one that Shirlè is engaged in.

George Major talked about putting forward a peace campaign that will be beneficial and unharmful to people. My conclusion is that people are becoming aware, and it is far better to help people awaken and become aware to this whole concept that things are going to change. People always change the mode of living and society. Look at what is happening now in eastern Europe. And look at China. Eventually they are going to change their society as well.

The more people that are ready for the New Awareness of Living, the more we will be able to change this whole concept of living. People are doing it now in all aspects, from the rainforests of Brazil, where people are campaigning to get part of the rainforest formed into a park so that we can always have some of that.

Also, people are more interested in using less chemicals on our fruits and vegetables. They stopped buying them and as a consequence that got attention. If people would stop buying things that are harmful, the economy would force change. People have the power if they stand together. Alone one falters, but when we are a strong voice we can do plenty. This is what George Major must have meant.

Toward the end of the séance, when George Major told about my meeting the new contact within six months, this actually came about when I met the shaman for the first time. It was in 1986 when I met the shaman, which was a good six months which took three years from the time of the séance with George Major. Of course, their years and their time is so off … whenever I've asked for things relating to time, I've found time is one concept you simply cannot ask a space person! They just do not dwell in time. Their time is continuous, as ours is; the only difference is we are *geared* by time.

As far as the reference made to Ralph Markin, there has only been one name which has come to me—George Markin—

who used to be a major and lived in Montreal. I have not met with this George Markin. In my search I contacted all of the spiritual churches in Montreal, in 1983, and did not receive one reply. Nobody bothered to even answer me. George Markin happens to be a psychic consultant, so it's possible he could be the one, I simply do not know.

Spirituality is the answer.
You must lead with your heart, not with your head.

Chapter 11

George Major Communicates

In February 1986, David MacKenzie-Thornton held another séance in Paris in which he succeeded at contacting George Major. The following is an extract from the tape recording. The conversation is between David and George Major, as we know him, from Sirius-B.

Date: February 22, 1986   **Location: Paris**

GEORGE MAJOR: Good evening. You know me as George Major.

DAVID: Oh really? Good evening, George. This is a very big surprise. I was thinking about you today. Good evening.

GEORGE MAJOR: I think we must take our time for those who have difficulty in following our conversation.

DAVID: It doesn't matter, George. It's very interesting. I have a particular reason for thinking it's very interesting ... but never mind, we'll tell it afterwards, if we have to.

GEORGE MAJOR: We ... I came recently, but was not really tied in to speak on matters which we wish to discuss this evening.

DAVID: Should we put the light out, George?

GEORGE MAJOR: Perhaps it matters ... yes.

DAVID: But you are speaking so well, so much better than you did when you first came to this little group.

GEORGE MAJOR: Yes. Also we have not manifested. We have on occasions been present. And have established a better contact and realigned our energies to make the contact less disturbing.

DAVID: Yes, that's what our friend Peter (said) ... a disturbing vibration. That's great.

GEORGE MAJOR: Now ... as you know, many of our colleagues and brothers have sent envoys to your planet. On occasions we have recovered the body of the resident who no longer desired to use it.

DAVID: Are these what we call walk-ins?

GEORGE MAJOR: Not precisely. The concept of walk-ins in your terminology amounts to that.

DAVID: That's what was done with the permission of the person ... in agreement with the person?

GEORGE MAJOR: On occasion, yes. It is _____ we are more interested in. Also, on occasions we have succeeded in manufacturing a clone, a copy of a physical being, which we can occupy.

DAVID: For as long as you wish?

GEORGE MAJOR: No, indeed. If it is a clone, that is to say a replica of the human entity, it is subject to the laws of humankind. The _____ has the limited life.

DAVID: Yes, you could use it for some years.

GEORGE MAJOR: Yes, yes. Now, a second lady who visited us on our last visit …

DAVID: Yes, Shirlè.

GEORGE MAJOR: Yes … was rather distressed at having lost her recent contact. The new contact is ready.

DAVID: Oh, she will be very, very happy to hear that.

GEORGE MAJOR: Indeed I believe she has already met this master.

DAVID: Yes, she told me she had met somebody, but she wasn't sure about it. And I asked Peter and Peter seemed to think that she ought to be very careful. Her situation has changed now, has it?

GEORGE MAJOR: Peter is not really linked with her activities. It is on a different plane of his knowledge. We believe that she can aid us in our world and your world. We have no intention, of course, of enslaving or controlling your world. We wish Earth _____ to acceptance … to have recognition. This is necessary before _____ emits out _____ of warning and guiding the peoples of the Earth to the dangers of that _____ development. I believe you are familiar with the results of the scientists of my planet.

DAVID: Yes, well, in a very general sense, George. A very general sense.

GEORGE MAJOR: The scientific developments have progressed beyond the nuclear …

DAVID: To the subnuclear …

GEORGE MAJOR: The subnuclear devices ... bombs are created which on the early tests worked well. One bomb was sufficient to annihilate the entire planet. No explosion took place at this instant greater of the material of the planet.

DAVID: Hm, that explains ...

GEORGE MAJOR: Simply the material ceased to exist and was transformed into energies. This, of course, included the residents of that planet.

DAVID: They were not killed, as we say? They were transformed?

GEORGE MAJOR: In the eyes of the majority of your world we were killed. But their physical bodies disappeared. However, the _____ of the nature of their dying, their etheric bodies continued. This new planet _____ itself as it was a planet _____ changed. _____ took place for a new evolution of beings.

DAVID: Oh which you are one?

GEORGE MAJOR: Yes, I am one. Several, many, many generations on home planet original ...

DAVID: You cannot tell me when in our time this happened? How many thousands ... millions of years ago?

GEORGE MAJOR: I would believe it was around the time of the birth of your religion.

DAVID: Jesus Christ? About 2,000 years?

GEORGE MAJOR: About 2,000 actually.

DAVID: You told me both times that you were a young man of 2,000 years.

GEORGE MAJOR: 1,500.

DAVID: 1,500, yes. I see, so you are almost first generation.

GEORGE MAJOR: I suppose I am at that.

DAVID: Almost, yes? But there are others who are, shall I say, born all the time?

GEORGE MAJOR: Exactly, yes.

DAVID: How are they born, George, by a matter of interest. Is it a mental process?

GEORGE MAJOR: It is, I suppose, by a mental process, somewhat as of your séance timbre. A spirit is _____ born. A materialized spirit.

DAVID: I see, yes. I would like you to give a particular message for our friend Shirlè because, as you probably know, I am supposed to be seeing her soon.

GEORGE MAJOR: A gentleman she has already met is one of our contacts, one of our agents.

DAVID: He is an Earth person?

GEORGE MAJOR: He is an Earth person.

DAVID: He has been contacted by you?

GEORGE MAJOR: Yes. We expect later to work the third quarter of your year … and she will meet her true agent through the agency of this gentleman.

DAVID: I see, yes. And can you tell me this gentleman's name? The one she is in contact with at the moment?

GEORGE MAJOR: I think it is Gordon.

DAVID: Gordon. I see, yes. You believe that, you're not entirely sure?

GEORGE MAJOR: I have still troubles with your system of naming.

DAVID: Yes, that's understandable. But she met him last year, didn't she? In our language.

GEORGE MAJOR: Recent … less than half of one of your years.

DAVID: Yes, six months … And this is the contact she has been waiting for?

GEORGE MAJOR: No, this is the contact to the contact.

DAVID: Yes, that's what I mean … the preliminary contact. Yes, I see. Oh, she'll be absolutely thrilled, George, to hear about this. Should I wait until I see her, or should I tell her now?

GEORGE MAJOR: It would not hurt. In fact, it might raise her spirits to tell her now. She appears a little depressed.

DAVID: Yes. Because she feels she has not made any progress?

GEORGE MAJOR: She feels she has not progressed when her last agent had to be withdrawn.

DAVID: Which was ... about two years ago, wasn't it? Yes, he had to be withdrawn because he was indiscreet, as you said?

GEORGE MAJOR: Yes.

DAVID: So, to all intents and purposes, he died.

GEORGE MAJOR: Yes.

DAVID: And he is now back with you, isn't he?

GEORGE MAJOR: Yes, he is. Having the _____ collector.

DAVID: I see, and will he be given another mission?

GEORGE MAJOR: Once we are sure, yes, that he is reliable.

DAVID: What happened there? I don't want all the details, but did he become rather, shall we say, blown up with his own importance in this field? Is that why he was indiscreet?

GEORGE MAJOR: Somewhat.

DAVID: He was contaminated by, what we say, earthly ambitions?

GEORGE MAJOR: Yes, started to talk to the public media.

DAVID: Which he was not supposed to do.

GEORGE MAJOR: It is not practical at the present state of affairs, but he still could have called on remembrances which could have been embarrassing to us.

DAVID: Yes.

GEORGE MAJOR: We do indeed have vehicles in your world.

DAVID: Oh, you do?

GEORGE MAJOR: They are hidden, but many of our agents know of that location.

DAVID: And what ... are these vehicles to be used in case of need to evacuate a certain number?

GEORGE MAJOR: Indeed, indeed.

DAVID: And they are physical vehicles?

GEORGE MAJOR: They are physical vehicles because in an emergency we would require to transport physical beings.

DAVID: Yes, yes. Where to and for how long is another matter, isn't it, George?

GEORGE MAJOR: Definitely.

DAVID: You can't have many people flying in a physical vehicle through space for very long, unless you have the right kind of physical support for them.

GEORGE MAJOR: Certainly.

DAVID: These are things which are difficult for us to even think about, aren't they?

GEORGE MAJOR: Yes, indeed.

DAVID: So there are physical vehicles ready in case of need?

GEORGE MAJOR: Yes. Now I think I shall leave you. Send

blessings to all.

DAVID: Yes, thank you very much. I'm so happy that you did come, particularly pleased that you are able to communicate so clearly now.

GEORGE MAJOR: It is better.

DAVID: Yes, very very good. Thank you so much, George. God bless you, as we say.

This next extract is from a séance on April 2, 1986. The conversation is between Yamani, a Hindu girl in spirit, who volunteered to go to Sirius-B, to test the conditions.

DAVID: I'm so glad to hear you because I'm hoping you will be able to tell me about the George Major situation. Have you been able to go?

YAMANI: Yes, I went.

DAVID: Oh, good. Good girl.

YAMANI: There is really much water there.

DAVID: Yes, that's what we thought. That's what he told us.

YAMANI: It's just a little bit of land, but is mostly water. But it is water of a different substance. It looks heavier than water. Even if you dive very deeply, the water pressure is very light. It's like the air. The deeper you go down, the lighter you become.

DAVID: That's curious, isn't it?

YAMANI: On your planet, the deeper you go, the more the

pressure of the water is heavy.

DAVID: Yes, it's the other way around.

YAMANI: The water is green.

DAVID: Green?

YAMANI: Green, like the grass. And there are all different creatures.

DAVID: What kind of creatures? We know that George Major himself looks rather like a porpoise ... sort of a dolphin.

YAMANI: Yes, they look like your dragons.

DAVID: Oh really?

YAMANI: But they're not nasty.

DAVID: They're lizards, are they?

YAMANI: Look like their cousins in the _____.

DAVID: With the long neck?

YAMANI: Yes and with four heads.

DAVID: Four heads, really?

YAMANI: Yes, all around, and they are all green.

DAVID: And they live in the water too, do they?

YAMANI: Yes, _____ creatures in the water. They have round houses in the water.

DAVID: Like bowls?

YAMANI: Yes, like bowls with windows in it.

DAVID: That's for George and his people, not for the other ... the animals.

YAMANI: They have all kinds of animals ... and they all look like animals ... _____ ... look like dogs, only swimming.

DAVID: They are all ... I was going to say human beings, but they are not human beings?

YAMANI: Well yes, they are human beings, but they don't look like human beings ... they are not animals.

DAVID: Do they all communicate with each other?

YAMANI: Yes. They have completely different races. On your planet you have white people, and you have yellow people, and you have black people and brown people. And you have Arabs and Africans and you have Chinese ...

DAVID: Yes, but here on Earth, although we may all have a different color of skin and our features may be rather different, we are all the same, really.

YAMANI: Yes, but there the features are very, very different. They can communicate with each other.

DAVID: They can? They all communicate with each other?

YAMANI: Yes.

DAVID: Not like here, where we have so many different languages.

YAMANI: You have a sort of coded language.

DAVID: A mental language?

YAMANI: And they all understand each other and they can communicate with each other. It is very interesting. They have all the different culture and different thinking, but they never have any wars.

DAVID: They never fight?

YAMANI: No, they have no battles. They're all peaceful.

DAVID: That's marvelous, isn't it? We hope that one day our Earth might be like that.

YAMANI: The human beings are too selfish ...

DAVID: How long did you stay there, Yamani? Enough to look around, anyway.

YAMANI: Yes, just quite a while.

DAVID: Did you see George himself?

YAMANI: Yes, I said hello to him, and he showed me everything around and he explained all that I tell you to.

DAVID: Did he say he was coming back to speak to us?

YAMANI: Yes.

DAVID: He comes in his mental body.

YAMANI: Yes.

DAVID: He stays at home, so to speak, and comes on the mental plane to communicate with us and with you ... Thank you so much, Yamani. If you think of anything more another time, you'll tell me, won't you?

YAMANI: Yes, I will.

DAVID: It may help us to understand the situation better because it's such a curious thing ... a curious situation, as far as we're concerned. It's something we have to think about a great deal, something very hard to understand, the way you describe it. I understand your words and your description, but the ideas behind it are difficult. I suppose it was a shock for you too, wasn't it?

YAMANI: Not a shock ... it was very unusual.

DAVID: Well, thank you so much, Yamani.

YAMANI: You're welcome. Say hello to our friends. *Bon soir. Excusez moi ...*

> **Date: May 4, 1986.**   **George Major in Paris**

GEORGE MAJOR: Good evening.

DAVID: Good evening, George Major.

GEORGE MAJOR: Indeed.

DAVID: Good evening, it's so nice to hear you. As you know, I've been hoping for another talk with you before I go to see our friends.

GEORGE MAJOR: I take this opportunity to send blessings to all our friends.

DAVID: Yes, thank you.

GEORGE MAJOR: Those who we have not met physically yet, also.

DAVID: You mean, on the other side of our ocean, I suppose.

GEORGE MAJOR: Yes.

DAVID: Yes, well, I'm going to complete the recording of our talks so far with this one, and let them hear it all, George. And I'm sure they'll be very happy and it will give rise to a great deal of discussion.

GEORGE MAJOR: I would indeed think it will. Perhaps you have questions.

DAVID: Yes. You don't mind me being frank, do you, George? I have three questions. I think one of them is probably less important than the others, so I'll start with that one. Our friend Yamani came to see you a little while ago. She said she would come back and tell me what it was like for her with you. She gave a very interesting description of it. What occurred to me is when your planet was dissolved, so to speak, into the etheric, you all took such different shapes ... you who resemble a dolphin ... your race ... the human race, I suppose? And the animals, who took all sorts of odd shapes, such as dragons.

GEORGE MAJOR: Indeed. We are not all indigenous to this planet.

DAVID: Oh really?

GEORGE MAJOR: It is a stage of evolution. Once one has passed beyond the incarnations on the material plane, one can reincarnate in a new cycle on the etheric plane.

DAVID: When you say the "material plane," you mean the earth plane?

GEORGE MAJOR: There are indeed other planets in the many solar systems.

DAVID: (On) that we must agree, yes. But you yourself, your race, was indigenous to Sirius-B?

GEORGE MAJOR: Many others ...

DAVID: But when, so to speak, in the physical on your planet, what shape ... what other physical shape did you have? Something like ours?

GEORGE MAJOR: Yes, indeed, we were somewhat humanoid. Somewhat larger than you.

DAVID: About twice our size?

GEORGE MAJOR: No, no. Two meters. We were _____, but they were _____.

DAVID: Why was that, because you were already living in the water, or close to it?

GEORGE MAJOR: We had most of our lives in the water. Indeed, yes. We were capable of pore (?) breathing, that is to say we could breathe in the waters or in the air.

DAVID: Either one or the other, it didn't matter to you.

GEORGE MAJOR: We had to reduce our—I don't know what you call them—rhythm—when we entered the waters.

As the extraction of the oxygen, _____ the oxygen was somewhat inferior to that of the air-based life.

DAVID: Your air-based life, on your planet?

GEORGE MAJOR: Yes.

DAVID: Land-based, you mean.

GEORGE MAJOR: Yes.

DAVID: There were other creatures on your planet in physical form?

GEORGE MAJOR: Indeed. There were many varieties of creatures, much as on your planet.

DAVID: But when you were transformed from your planet to the etheric by this nuclear explosion, or non-explosion as you say, you took different shapes because you had to live in the water?

GEORGE MAJOR: Yes.

DAVID: Well, what you considered to be the water, which is the etheric form of water.

GEORGE MAJOR: Indeed. The change produced an aura of intense radiation which caused mutations ... even at the etheric levels. To protect ourselves from the worst of these radiations, we had to enter into _____. After one or two generations, as rapid as that, the cross-mutation became _____ —and our form changed to adapt to obliterate disease (?).

DAVID: I see, and this was the same for the other creatures on your planet at that time? They all changed to the new circumstances?

GEORGE MAJOR: You will understand that the etheric is somewhat more pliable than the physical. The mutation was able to take place in two generations. Indeed, mutations that occur within one lifetime.

DAVID: Very quick.

GEORGE MAJOR: Indeed.

DAVID: Well, we mustn't spend all the time on this one, George. But to come to that point when you said not everyone is indigenous to your planet, but some other forms of life come in as part of the process of evolution, why is that? Is yours a particularly favored spot in the universe? Is it a question of attraction?

GEORGE MAJOR: There is indeed not a great many natural etheric planets. It is a somewhat favored spot. However, there are etheric entities on physical planets, but this is not entirely favorable to them. I have already spoken of this, that there are etheric and astral beings. Also on your own planet you can find some etheric beings.

DAVID: Why are they here on our planet?

[BREAK]

DAVID: ... physical body for a time. They are the ones who would know.

GEORGE MAJOR: There are indeed two or three ships secret (?) on your planet. They could be indeed totally insufficient to evacuate any quantity of persons.

DAVID: What would they be used for?

GEORGE MAJOR: They offer indeed no intention to evacuate persons.

DAVID: What would they be used for? To get Betelgeuse people back to their … _____?

GEORGE MAJOR: No, they were transporting equipment. They are observation … they are not evacuation ships.

DAVID: So they will never leave, or you can't say, I suppose. It depends on circumstances?

GEORGE MAJOR: Yes … I see no practicality in trying to evacuate a large quantity of people.

DAVID: No, no, that makes very good sense, George, because in any event, our make-up is very different …

GEORGE MAJOR: Indeed, indeed, yes.

DAVID: To evacuate hundreds of people, or thousands of people, you would need all that quantity of physical food. The problem is so enormous that it cannot be realized.

GEORGE MAJOR: Indeed. In the event of catastrophe we may try, indeed, to evacuate a representative number of people, so that the human race could possibly continue on another planet.

DAVID: You would have to find another planet that is similar to the earth, wouldn't you? As far as atmosphere and general conditions are concerned. But that would be only the ultimate trial. After the catastrophe.

GEORGE MAJOR: Yes.

DAVID: And any of that, as far as I can judge, it would mean that these people that you were able to evacuate would have to live and reproduce on this other planet for thousands of years. When the earth could be reinhabited, they could come back and start it all over again here, because the earth would be laid waste, would it not? If it remained in its physical form.

GEORGE MAJOR: In its physical form it would be out of action for ... 3,000 years, we calculate.

DAVID: Well, just one more question before you take over properly, if we have the time, George. This recent accident that our Russian friends ... I call them our friends ... have had last week, a week ago ... that doesn't cut into your sphere, does it? It's not serious enough.

GEORGE MAJOR: It is in itself not serious, but as the _____ ... go wrong, but this anti-_____ or incompetence, it shows where your world is headed. It does not of necessity have to be an intentional confrontation.

DAVID: No, it can either be an industrial use of the energy or the military use of it.

GEORGE MAJOR: Yes. That experiment went too far.

DAVID: Well, thank you very, very much, George. If you have any other things you want to tell me, I'll be very happy to listen.

GEORGE MAJOR: We are trying to let more agents onto your world. As I said before, we do hope to make contact in person with your planet. We thank them greatly for their help and hope they will continue there. There aren't many of us from many planets and we take the planet _____, but this is not relevant time to go into mentalitic and bodily differences ... are different races. We are trying to _____ ... telepathic contact, and hope in the near future to see this possible. ... very sensitive to these contacts, and we hope that she soon will be ... to receive messages ... and ... not ourselves so reliant on contacts without agents. Much work to do. There is still much work to be done. Our work is indeed urgent. The disaster that will come has not been determined ... is still a possibility that it is way off ... but not personally and one should not still _____ ... as possible. We send our blessings and gratitude for our participants and our thanks.

DAVID: Yes, they will certainly hear that, George. I have asked my friend Shirlè, if she can, to find a trance medium to be available to us in the event you can come to talk to them direct.

GEORGE MAJOR: Excellent idea. I will certainly do my utmost to make contact. And now we are more experienced in the contact. Disturbing to this medium.

DAVID: I will take your music with me. It does help.

GEORGE MAJOR: Bless you, indeed. Blessings and peace for your world.

I never met anybody by the name of Gordon, as George Major mentioned in the earlier séance. The only thing I can think it could be is Jorgen, whom I met at the 1988 Jorpah in Seattle. In the séance George Major admitted he wasn't that good at names. The reason they have so much trouble with naming is because they know a person by their vibration and not their name. Names are unimportant to them. Jorgen turned to me and said, "I see you are writing your book."

I told him, "Well, I'm not exactly writing it. I'm having help from Ann Ulrich, who is an author."

He said, "You're writing it. She's just doing all that which you are writing."

I looked at him and I didn't say anything. Then I asked him, "Can you tell me why I was given this injection in the back of my neck when I was really thoroughly angry about it?"

He said, "Don't get angry. We had to do that." So, he seemed to know a lot. He seemed to know me. He looked at me and he said, "You're doing well, we're very pleased with you," so perhaps Gordon is Jorgen. But this meeting was in 1988, so the timing wasn't right.

Again, George Major may have made a mistake. He may be a spirit and know a lot of things, but what if he isn't perfect either?

We're not perfect on this earth plane, so why must we believe they are perfect wherever they are?

I believe the shaman is my contact. I haven't had any other contacts who have given me the information. Most the people I have met have received information from me. Jorgen and the shaman are the only ones, so far, who have given me information.

Chapter 12

Kromme Speaks

An attempt was made to contact George Major from Sirius-B in a seance held in Canada on May 21, 1986. When David MacKenzie-Thornton came for a visit from Paris, we located a medium who does channeling. Her name is Heather Woodhams. She and her husband George live in Aldergrove, B.C.

What follows are portions of the transcript of this séance and two others that followed, containing information pertinent to my situation. Kromme is the entity or guide who comes through Heather.

Date: Wednesday, May 21, 1986
Location: Aldergrove, B.C., Canada

GEORGE W.: We're gathered with a group of friends, as you're aware. Do you have any place that you would like to begin, given that you know the main thrust of the evening—the main interest—in having who is called George Major join us this evening? Would you like to begin—and take off?

KROMME: George Major is not here as of this moment. I have been told that he will come. However, we shall just wait and see. There is a desperation with Shirlè that she must release. Contacts are made when it is time for them to be made. We realize that the days are so important on your side, and it seems so long since the last contact. However, on our side time is irrelevant, and so much time on your side slips by, and it seems eternal to you. There is much work to be done on our side, and contact

160

is only made when it is necessary—not just for a friendly visit. So Shirlè must be patient. As I explained to you and Heather in channeling last night, the entity that touched Heather's shoulder was from the other side—an alien— and he is associated with George Major. However, he is a very quiet entity, and is learning (understanding?) in the distance. He is allowing his presence to be known by the touch. He is seldom felt. How shall I explain to you when I am close to Heather—she feels my presence? She feels that, as if another human were in the room. I am able to transmit to her a density as a human has, and so she can feel me. This entity was able to manifest himself—or shall I say—itself to her so that she was aware of it. However, it does not have the density, and is not able at this point to make the density to be easily felt. And that is why she was not aware of its presence at that time—until it actually touched her shoulder. Unlike myself—though she is able to feel when I am in the same room with her—this entity is around Shirlè. In time she will begin to know it, and she will feel his presence as it becomes more familiar to her.

GEORGE W.: Do you have a name for this individual?

KROMME: I do not have a name. I have a feeling—the chord is C—that is all I can tell you. That's all he's telling me. It is almost dragon like. It is very large, and has scaly skin. I can only tell you those details. It is a gentle, very peaceful entity. I am convinced that it is friendly, and it is trustworthy at this point. There is no communication. There is no message from it to Shirlè, other than it is there for her. When there is important messages to come through he will communicate—or shall I correct myself— it will communicate.

GEORGE W.: How will that communication be made, Kromme?

KROMME: The communication will be made numerous different ways. It can be made through it touching her if she will relax and allow her sensitivity to become more aware instead of worrying so much about what is going to happen. She mustn't worry. Communication sometimes can be made through dreams, and other means if Shirlè is unable to hear what is being told to her. This entity is aware that you are channeling, and messages can come through Heather. As you are aware, George, this has happened many times before. We have given you messages for other people. This is correct, is it not?

GEORGE W.: That's correct, Kromme. You or Heather—I'm not sure—the voice sounds really strained. Is everything all right?

KROMME: Everything is fine. Heather asked tonight that I use my own voice, or as close as I was able to get to. If David prefers to hear the voice of the entity who is speaking, as we explained to you _____ channeling, sometimes it is more important to people for verification to hear different voices. We do not feel that this is necessary when we are just channeling with you and Heather, as you within yourselves know that there are different entities here talking. We are doing this simply for verification of those in the room.

GEORGE W.: You do sound strained, more so than normal. That's why I was asking, Kromme. Heather's voice is so much deeper. Perhaps David has a question, if that's all right?

KROMME: That is fine.

DAVID: Good evening, Kromme.

KROMME: Good evening, David.

DAVID: I am very happy to be able to join this little circle and make your acquaintance. Have you—did you say just now that this new entity was attuned to our chord of C?

KROMME: Yes. Could you speak quietly, please? Yes, it is attuned to the musical chord of middle C.

DAVID: Middle C—yes. And would it be a good thing for future meetings to have a little music in that chord to start off with?

KROMME: Yes. You might attempt to call it by the—using the music as you have with George Major.

DAVID: Do you think that there is the danger attached to that chording?

KROMME: No. However, it is up to the entity that is being called as to whether they wish to come forward. Sometimes they choose not to come. I am not always certain as to why they make this choice, myself, as I am in close attunement to Heather and George, and I am here for their spiritual guidance and their development, and to help them develop in their channeling. I am always here for them. However, there are times when I have attempted to contact other guides which they are interested in speaking to, and they have not always come forward, and I have not always been able to find out the reasons why they have not come forward.

DAVID: Yes. So we usually say, or think, that it is because the conditions aren't quite right for them to come. However, this question of Sirius-B—the contact with George Major—is a rather special case. Is it not, Kromme?

KROMME: Yes. We would agree with you, and that is why we agreed to channel tonight.

DAVID: Yes.

GEORGE W.: May I ask why it is a special case?

KROMME: Are you asking me?

GEORGE W.: Yes.

KROMME: We feel that there is much information to come through regarding their ESP—because of the safety factor of your own planet. As we explained to you last night, we feel that you have the technology available to get involved in some atomic disasters such as happened on your planet, and we feel that within seven years (by '93) you will be able to do this. We feel that these entities will be able to give you much more detailed information and warning than I myself am able to give you, as that is not my specialty, and I have had very limited involvement up to this time. This is why we feel that it is important.

DAVID: Yes. You are very happy to cooperate with George Major and his people?

KROMME: Yes. They have convinced me that they are peaceful entities and they have no interest in taking over your earth plane.

DAVID: That is what George Major told me the last time I spoke with him. He spoke of certain extraterrestrial people who were not friendly to us on this earth. But you are convinced that he is friendly?

KROMME: I am convinced that he is friendly. I must admit that I have not had an encounter with those who are not friendly. I have had some contact with aliens, but for the majority of my time I have been involved in earthlings. So I am not an expert in this field. But George Major has been able to convince me that there is no danger from his planet. I should correct myself. I have not spoken to him. Specifically, I have spoken to the entity that answers to Middle C.

DAVID: Oh yes, yes. Do you think you will be able yourself to look at conditions on this planet with the help of Middle C?

KROMME: I might consider going. I was shown last night. Heather was involved in this—the disaster that happened there some years ago. I had only seen it from a distance, as she did, when the earth—if you wish to use that term, or the planet—became liquefied. It also became much smaller in size—had changed color. That is my total knowledge. I was there with Heather and with George the night—Friday night—when we went to see you, and I did hear the tapes. The young lady from India who went there—she described the dragon-like creatures.

DAVID: Yes, it's four heads?

KROMME: I would say that Middle C fits into this classification. However, he only has three.

DAVID: Three heads?

KROMME: Yes.

GEORGE W.: Would Middle C—is he with us this evening, and …

KROMME: He is here. He is not willing to talk through Heather. He may answer questions. If you have some, I will relay them to him—or shall I say, he can hear you himself—he may relay the answers through me.

DAVID: May I ask where Middle C is to be attached—is to attach himself to this group here, to this part of the world—rather than George Major?

KROMME: Yes. He is for this group, in this part of the world. He is not—he has not been here longer than your _____ period of five months. He is still fairly insecure— to use one of your earth terms—and he is still attempting to fit into your vibrations, which is very difficult for him as he is so differently attuned from you earthlings. I suppose I should include myself in that. However, I must admit I do feel I'm a little higher.

DAVID: You are from our ... you are not from ... Kromme?

KROMME: I am an entity who is evolved from your earth. That is why I _____ myself just a little finer tuned—shall we say—than those still on Earth.

DAVID: Yes, of course. Yes. Look, are we to hear direct from this Middle C, or from George Major tonight, do you think? Or should we ask the questions through you?

KROMME: I do not have the indication that George Major will arrive. Middle C will be willing to answer questions that he is able to. He has told me that it will be at least seven months more (to December '86) in your Earth terms before he is comfortable communicating directly through Heather or Shirlè.

DAVID: Yes, seven months, yes. Well, should this group here, in this particular place—this particular town—should they try to meet or arrange for you, rather, for Heather and George to have a regular meeting on their account, so that questions, if necessary, can be asked of Middle C?

KROMME: We feel at this time—or shall I say, my own personal opinion regarding Heather's channeling is—that the humans belonging—or that surround themselves with Shirlè—are attuned so far from Heather that she would find it extremely difficult to have a total relaxation, and a very successful channeling with numbers of them around. If there are questions that are wanting to be asked, she might phone George, and he could ask them from time to time, if there are messages that are important they get—that they get to her, then we shall arrange for them to come through in George and Heather's regular channeling. And Shirlè will be contacted regarding this. There may be situations in which one or more of the members of that group may be asked to be present for information to be given, possibly information that only they would understand. And so therefore it would be important for them to be present. However, we do not see this mandatory for a period of time yet. We would like to notify Shirlè that there are space ships around constantly, watching the skies and watching the peoples. At this point in time, I, myself, Kromme, feel along with the entities that I am involved with—which I might add, totals a little over 2,000 entities that I have constant contact with—we are all of the feeling that the negative on your earth plane has been sped up. And we feel that there are many upcoming disasters which Heather and George have been told about. These aliens will be here to help alleviate, and to help save some of your humanity. It is impossible for us, or anyone on our side, to give an exact time of impending disaster, or to give you the exact results of this disaster. It is because it is never predetermined. There are so many encompassing factors that must be taken into consideration, and we do our best to analyze them. However, any predictions that are made are not 100 percent foolproof. As we have explained to George, if you are having a game of cards involving numerous people, you can analyze the cards the people probably will lay down and play. However, from time to time, there is one individual who will decide to just sway from their normal pattern, and this will change the whole play. So this is why predictions are not always 100 percent foolproof.

DAVID: Yes. Well, I think we understand that fair enough, Kromme. Haven't you mentioned questions from Shirlè's group? Would it be in order for George to ask the question that he has written down—a question which Shirlè herself would have liked to ask, but in this case George can ask for her? Would that be in order?

KROMME: Yes, he may ask this question.

GEORGE W.: Or would you mind if Shirlè asks, or would you prefer my question?

KROMME: We would prefer that you asked, George.

GEORGE W.: I shall light a candle if you don't mind, Kromme. [*A 32-second pause here while George lights a candle.*] Shirlè is having some degree of insecurities. Perhaps if there is something you could give her information wise, it could reassure her as to your closeness, your measure of responsiveness to her or her group.

KROMME: At this point in time Middle C is constantly with the group, watching them, and listening to them—the closeness as I explained before. Shirlè must relax, and stop being so desperate for information. If she could learn to relax, and even to meditate more peacefully, telepathic communication can be made. It is being blocked by her, and by the desperation of the group. There is nothing very important or desperate to get through at this time. But telepathic communication would be made if she would just relax. That could be her reassurance. However, it is something that she will have to work at.

GEORGE W.: Is there some physical thing that Shirlè or perhaps one or two others in the group who are perhaps sensitive to it, could get involved in, toning per se, or like thing, in conjunction with the meditation?

KROMME: Toning would be very ideal for that group, from my observations when I was there this past Friday night with you, and with Heather. There is an awful lot of hypertension involved in that group. I classified it as desperation to communicate. Toning will help them relax. They must not be like the people in the '50s who ran out and built bomb shelters, convinced that there was going to be a bomb, and they were desperate. They must relax with the situation. They have not been left high and dry. Communication will be made. Middle C is going to communicate telepathically, not complicated messages, but just to let them know that he is there. There is nothing to be said—other than that—to them at this time. I am sorry to be so repetitious.

GEORGE W.: One last thing, Kromme, and I explained to Shirlè that you may not appreciate the question if you even were in the position to receive it. She was asking about a present that had been acquired for her on another planet. Do you, or does Middle C, have any knowledge of, and if so could they tell us about it?

KROMME: All I am being shown now is a bright light. I am _____ from this sunlight—this bright light that I am being shown—that this gift coming from a different planet would be—will mean a total enlightening—be a totally enlightening experience for Shirlè. It will open up her eyes, and she will understand more what is going on. That is the only communication that I am receiving in answer to that question.

GEORGE W.: Either that's what she was looking for, or not, only she knows—so we won't pursue it any further. Thank you, Kromme. Is there anything else, David, that you would like to ... such as ...

DAVID: I would like to ask Middle C, Kromme, whether my own, or our own contacts in France with George Major is to continue?

KROMME: Yes, we have a communication that it will continue. But it will not continue on a regular basis, and it will not continue for a long period of time.

DAVID: No, no, well, it has not been regular, but I think it has been very helpful in the event toward this group here.

KROMME: I would agree with that.

DAVID: Will there be a _____ is George Major hurting to give further information for a limited time? Am I right in understanding you that way?

KROMME: Yes, he is.

DAVID: I see, and then we should hear, then, more from him.

KROMME: Middle C has indicated to me that George Major

is—to put it in your Earth terms—like a supervisor. He is bringing suitable entities from his planet to yours, and introducing them to humanoids, so that they might watch and guide them, and attempt to interfere—any nuclear holocausts that are able to happen in the near future. He is to _____ the entity. And when he has all arrangements made with other entities, he will then withdraw, as he has other jobs that he is involved with.

DAVID: Yes. Thank you very much. I thought it might be that way when I heard about Middle C from Heather in the first place. Thank you very much.

KROMME: Shirlè, do you have any questions? If you do, would you please ask them very quietly?

SHIRLÈ: Thank you very much, Kromme. I guess as soon as Middle C contacts me, I will get my directions as to what I have to do next. Or do I still gather people, make the groups large, or have the groups small so we can meditate and get to know one another so we can be a strong entity? Is that advisable?

KROMME: You are much more able to accomplish things if you attract people of the same vibration. The UFO Society—I would suggest—could be broken into different nucleuses. Those of like vibrations—those that you feel comfortable with. It seemed to me the other night that there were numerous different vibrations—some of them quite shattering and destructive. I would suggest that those whom you feel most comfortable with, gather together, and grow together, and learn together, and share together. Do try to do toning. In meditation you will find communication far easier if you are of like vibration, and of like mind. You may suggest that those—I would say that there are between three and five different vibrations in your largest group at this time, not including others than those that were there on the Friday night. I would suggest that you suggest to them that you merge together in groups of like minds instead of becoming one large group which is very difficult to function with, and to accomplish anything. That is just from my perspective. Do you understand? You are, of course, free to do as you feel best.

GEORGE W.:   May I suggest, Kromme, that perhaps—not meaning to cut Shirlè off at the moment, but regarding that particular situation—perhaps we could arrange a time in the next week or two, or three, as is convenient to—some of these specifics be worked out, but not necessarily at this time.

KROMME: I have given my suggestions to Shirlè, and now a few meditations, she will get more—more information. It is now up to her to what she does.

SHIRLÈ: I'd like to ask you, Kromme—about a couple of weeks ago I'd come to that decision _____ _____ gathering people of the same vibration—as you say— that are wanting very much to meditate and to elevate themselves. And this is what we're going to be doing. So I thank you very much for suggesting, because that is what we are going to be doing.

KROMME: You will find that if you do accomplish this, and you relax with it, you will grow together spiritually, and you will be able to open up to receive, to do your own channeling—not necessarily the way that Heather does— but just through meditation. Messages will come through you. Entities on our side—entities from other planets— aliens—they are very able to telepathically communicate. The trance medium is only needed when your receiving signals are not working correctly. If you are totally in tune with yourself and the God-Force—or the Tao as I prefer to call Him—you will be able to receive telepathically quite easily.

SHIRLÈ: Thank you very much.

DAVID: May I ask you one last question, Kromme?

KROMME: Yes, you may.

DAVID: How are we to expect messages from entities from other planets—other planets other than Sirius-B?

KROMME: Yes, there will be numerous entities from other planets attempting to communicate with people such as yourself. It is very important in my estimation that you protect yourself before each channeling session. Your guides—your entities—your guardian angels—whichever term fits most comfortable with you, will insure that only positive will come through. However, if you are not careful, and you are willing to accept any entity, you may find yourself in a very uncomfortable situation.

DAVID: Yes, I heartily agree, but I asked the question because George Major mentioned certain entities, or certain people of certain planets who are not benevolent towards us, and it is up to us to try to find out whether they are in fact benevolent, or whether they are not. It's not easy for us. I think the only way we can do it is through our guides such as yourself.

KROMME: Each individual has a guide who is responsible for the spirituality of those people on your side. It is our job to insure that no negative comes through to you. However, we can only do this with your permission. If you are willing to open yourself up to anything and anyone, then we cannot stop this from happening. And so this is why I said it is so important that you ask before each session, that only positive entities respective of the God-Force, or of the Tao be allowed to come through.

DAVID: Yes. Thank you very much.

SHIRLÈ: Kromme, can I ask another question?

KROMME: Yes, you may.

SHIRLÈ: I still—y'know—have the eight plates that I was given, and I took them out of the bank because I felt that the bank wasn't that safe or secure. And I'm keeping them in a safe place. I still have not—only one person has deciphered it. I still don't know what it really, actually means.

KROMME: Shirlè, it is like communication with the entities on our side. It is not important for you at this time to know what it means. It is a gift—it is a gift from an entity, and you are to be honoured by this gift, and keep it safely. You have made a wise decision. When one is meant to have something, they will hold onto it, and as long as you respect and value this gift, it will remain with you no matter where you keep it. Until the time of upcoming disaster, you will not be made aware of the actual importance of these plates. However, they are involving space ships which I do feel you are quite aware of.

SHIRLÈ: Yes, I am. Thank you, you're most kind.

Date: May 27, 1986   Location: Aldergrove, B.C., Canada

KROMME: Middle C is here. You may continue. He will wait—

whatever you wish ..... You may talk with him through me. He at this point has not mastered your language. You would not be able to comprehend anything that he has to say. This is why you will be between six and seven months before he's really able to communicate. He feels it will take him that period of time before he can be understood.

DAVID: Rather like George Major at the beginning, Kromme.

KROMME: Yes. However, from the tapes that I heard of George Major, he is very well spoken compared to Middle C.

DAVID: Oh! Now! Yes, but in the beginning it was very difficult. I would just like to welcome Middle C into this little circle, which is not my circle but it is sort of a—I am a guest here that—which they welcomed—friend.

KROMME: He has informed me that he will be joining you from time to time in your circle.

DAVID: In the other ... in my country?

KROMME: Yes. Before he becomes firmly established here, he will be shown many different groups throughout the world to see their way of communication, and their way of life so that he establishes a sensitivity for the complete Earth, and understanding more fully its politics and its workings.

DAVID: Yes, well that is good. May I ask whether any of these groups are in Russia?

KROMME: Yes, there are some groups in Russia. It is very difficult for them to operate because of their political situation, but there are some secret test ones. I have been told there is a very strong group in Berlin.

DAVID: In East Berlin as reported.

KROMME: Yes, in East Berlin. And in Moscow there are numerous smaller, less developed groups throughout the countryside of Russia.

DAVID: Who are concerned with the space—with the aliens?

KROMME: Yes, they are concerned with the aliens. The aliens are particularly concerned with the Russians as they feel that they do not have quite the social conscience—shall I say—that other parts of the world have, and their space development program is progressing very rapidly. So the aliens are attempting to make as many people aware within Russia and the East Bloc countries as possible, so that they can develop the moral social conscience. However, just because of the political workings of those countries, it is extremely difficult for the average individual to really have much interference on the government.

DAVID: Much influence, you mean?

KROMME: Right. I'm sorry.

DAVID: Yes. Yes. It must be very difficult and heart-rending for them.

KROMME: Yes.

GEORGE W.: What is the specific purpose for Middle C and George Major's presence being here?

KROMME: They are here to make a _____ aware of the amount of nuclear development and the technical _____ technological advances being made within the earth plane these days. Also to make them aware of the potential direction in which they are aiming, which is the possible self destruction of humanity. However, there will be interference to stop this, as if mankind themselves are not willing to step in and hold it, then we hope that other means will be used. Presently I am not allowed to release that information, but there will have to be steps taken to stop this from happening. The aliens are here as a support for your peoples, as they feel that by an awareness program they will help—this will help shall we say—the human, the general populace, the governments' conscience. We realize in East Bloc countries it is very difficult for this to happen. However, in the Western countries this is a distinct possibility, and there is a certain amount of Western propaganda that does seep into the East Bloc countries.

DAVID: Yes. It is very urgent, isn't it, Kromme?

KROMME: Yes, it is very urgent. You've really no idea how urgent it is. Seven years may seem like such a long time. However, seven years goes by very quickly in your Earth terms.

DAVID: Seven years—yes. Well, we shall have to persevere and cooperate with the aliens so far as we can, provided they are the benevolent ones. _____ _____ _____ _____ _____ who are not benevolent might be interested in creating havoc on our Earth.

KROMME: You must keep in mind that the benevolent ones are here to help, and they will do their utmost to prevent those who are not benevolent from destroying your humanity as well.

DAVID: Yes, yes.

GEORGE W.: If I may, David—Shirlè, if I'm not mistaken— mentioned something about being taken away, picked up, transported off the planet. Is that correct, or is there any comment from them?

KROMME: Humanoids will be taken from the planet for a temporary period of time as I have been informed. But they will be returned to the planet after disasters have happened. As I have told you in numerous channelings, we do see your Earth slipping its axis and changing its face, and there will be much destruction. Many of you will be directed to the pockets as you call it in this side of the country—or safety areas—and are of the knowledge of what is going on. Many others will be brought in to you through numerous disasters, like being stranded, train wrecks, or plane crashes, and survivors will land on your door step. Others will be transported there by spacecraft. However, there will be those who will be there to the very end of time, and they will only have seconds to get from the face of the earth, and there will be no time for them to be taken to the pockets, so they must be taken to other safe areas and returned to the pockets when things have settled. That is the only information that I have been given.

DAVID: When you say other safe areas, Kromme, are you referring possibly to other planets?

KROMME: Yes, I am referring to other planets.

DAVID: And they have found other planets that could support our human life?

KROMME: There would be temporary arrangements made for short-term support of human life.

DAVID: But not for very much of it?

KROMME: No. There is no way we would be taking—shall I say the aliens would be taking—numerous groups of people, but would be some. But they do not have access to millions of spacecraft.

DAVID: No. So most of this one is—or if this disaster comes— the vast majority of the human, animal, insect population of this planet will be wiped out.

KROMME: Yes, it will.

DAVID: So there can only be possibly a few hundred, or at most a few thousand people saved from this ..... (*sound of tape recorder shutting off here*). May I change the tape over?

GEORGE W.: He's not unfamiliar with that. Kromme's not unfamiliar.

DAVID: No, no, but we don't like it, do we? All right, I think we're all right now again.

KROMME: We see that there are numerous pockets or safety areas spread throughout the world to which people will be directed. A rough estimation of people surviving the possible upcoming disasters, and I do say possible—we feel that they will be probably subject to change—would be in the estimation somewhere of three million people. (The present Earth population—as of July 6, 1986 channel 12 newsbreak is five billion people.)

DAVID: In the whole world?

KROMME: Of the whole world.

DAVID: Yes. That is including those who might be able to go away to another planet?

KROMME: Yes, that would be a modest amount of people.

DAVID: Yes, yes. Three million in all?

KROMME: Yes.

DAVID: Yes, well ...

GEORGE W.: David mentioned a possible time slot of 200 years for what you're talking about. Is this one of those possible that there's more than one eventuality, or ...

KROMME: Are you speaking about the slipping of the axis?

DAVID: My information related directly—as far as I remember—to the nuclear threat.

KROMME: Are you speaking of the nuclear wars that ... Could you be a little more specific for me?

DAVID: Well, I don't think I can say whether it was the nuclear war, or the nuclear accident, or the nuclear experimental threat.

KROMME: The information that I have received is that your scientists will have access to the subnuclear information in seven years (1993). However, we do not foresee them using this at this point. We do have the predictions that has come through Heather and George before—are that in 1992-1993 there will be a war involving most of the world. However, there will just be one nuclear bomb dropped and the rest of it will be regular warfare. There will be great damage through the one nuclear bomb, and many lives are lost through the rest of the war. Then we see in about 1995-1996 the slipping of the axis which will do a great amount of damage and devastate the face of the earth, destroying most of humanity. From there, there will be a ten-year isolation and the cleansing of the (sea?).

DAVID: A collapsing? Oh, a cleansing. This one nuclear bomb— will that be subnuclear?

KROMME: No. It will be nuclear as they have them now.

DAVID: Not a very brilliant prospect, is it, Kromme?

KROMME: No, it is extremely devastating for us on our side to watch what is happening on your side.

GEORGE W.: Is this whole thing part of what Middle C is here for then?

KROMME: He is here so that he can watch what is going on and he can be of assistance in this time of upcoming disasters. These aliens also just want to insure that your—mankind does not lose sight of the outcome if one person pushes a button to have a nuclear bomb go off. There must somewhere be a conscience for the receiving people not to reciprocate and destroy all of humanity on the earth.

DAVID: That is asking a lot, isn't it, Kromme?

KROMME: Yes, it is.

DAVID: So the chances are that there will be an enormous—in our language—an enormous influx of spirit to your side from our side.

KROMME: Yes, there will be. From my perspective I wonder who will be the best off, those who come to our side, or those who remain on your side.

DAVID: Exactly, but in any event this will mean an enormous amount of work for you to receive these people.

KROMME: Yes. It will be a shock to all concerned. Only those who are aware of the safety areas and aware of what the possible upcoming disasters are, will be—shall be the best off, even though they will endure much hardship—physical and emotional. They must be strong to receive those people who are—shall we say—dumped in their lap, and those who have no idea as to what is going on. And they will be going through great emotional trauma as well as possible physical injuries from the wars and the disasters.

DAVID: And those who come to your side—this _____ _____ will be in great—in a state of shock, too. And you will have to cope with them—you people—you spirits.

KROMME: Yes, we will be equally busy.

DAVID: They will, in fact, be dumped on you in the sense of the way, won't they?

KROMME: Yes, they will be. It will be extremely difficult for us to be attentive to all concerned so that they do not—shall we say—haunt your earth plane.

DAVID: Which plane?

KROMME: Your earth plane. And therefore not accomplishing, or growing, or developing, just wasting—in any empty void.

DAVID: Yes.

GEORGE W.: Other than the transportation of some peoples during this time of upset we talk about, what is the orientation of the groups involved in the UFOs?

KROMME: They must be—they must—the UFOs or the aliens—shall we say—must have contact in groups that can work with these aliens if there are things that must be done. I have not really given any specifics. However, I was just informed of another possible job that these UFOs might be involved in. If it appears that a nuclear holocaust might happen, they might just escort some of the planes carrying the nuclear bombs to lead out of our atmosphere into a void area in the universe for them to explode there, and do as little damage as possible.

GEORGE W.: Interesting concept, eh?

DAVID: That's a new concept. They would have to take them a long way from this Earth, wouldn't they?

KROMME: Yes, they would.

DAVID: And not near a—isolate them as you say—in a void area, where they would do little damage to other bodies in space.

KROMME: There are—there is a Black Hole, I have been informed. It is not too distant from your solar system, and they could be safely funneled into there.

GEORGE W.: That being a matter of a split-second application?

KROMME: Yes, it would be. This would confuse the scientists— somewhat at least.

DAVID: Indeed yes.

GEORGE W.: It's a rather understatement, I think, Kromme. Is there anything that Middle C or George Major through Middle C wants to get through to Shirlè and her group, or anyone in the group?

KROMME: We just feel that Shirlè must keep the groups small. Do meditation as we suggested to her, and try not to sensationalize what is happening, as the aliens, if they wanted anything to be sensationalized, they could certainly accomplish this on their own.

DAVID: You mean Shirlè and her group should keep fairly quiet about it all for the moment?

KROMME: Yes, they should. The general populace is not ready for this information and—shall we say—numerous thrill seekers would love to get as much information as possible, but it is not a positive situation. It is just a thrill-seeking situation.

> BEEP — BEEP
> BEEP — BEEP

GEORGE W.: Skip it, Kromme. (*The reading was terminated abruptly.*)

(One minute of silence here, followed by a four-second long beep. The 60-minute microcassette at slow speed ran out at this point.)

Chapter 13

Recruiting Helene

During the first week of November 1988, I flew from Vancouver down to Grand Junction, Colorado, where I spent two days with Ann Ulrich, who was then living forty miles south in Delta. We had met at the Rocky Mountain Conference for UFO Investigation the summer before, in Laramie, Wyoming. This conference has been put on every year since 1981 at the University of Wyoming by Dr. R. Leo Sprinkle, well known psychologist and UFO investigator.

It was at the 1988 conference that the two of us began to play with the idea of a book. Ann, who is in her late thirties, is another associate director for UFO Contact Center International. On top of being a housewife, the mother of three boys, and working two part-time jobs, she manages to find time for her esoteric work and her writing. Her first novel, *Intimate Abduction,* had just been published two months before. During my brief visit to Ann's home we interviewed intensely and I felt quite drained by the end of my visit.

Leaving Grand Junction at the crack of dawn, I flew to Phoenix, Arizona, where Helene picked me up. She wasn't feeling well. She was having trouble with her back. We drove to Safford, Arizona, where I spent two weeks with Helene. The first week we spent around her home and work place, and the second week we drove to Sedona, where we met another contactee. While in Sedona, we attended a conference called "Where the Eagles Gather." Two people there were in contact with the Ashtar Command. There were others there who spoke about dolphins and the Bell Rock in Sedona, plus more.

One of the main reasons I went to see Helene was because she was having a difficult time. She had been involved in a car accident in Las Vegas, September 1984, which had done damage to her spine. The doctors couldn't operate on her because she was too close to being permanently paralyzed. Poor Helene had been in almost constant pain from that very day. It was at the point where Helene had to take drugs for the pain, and she felt she was becoming addicted to the drugs. In fact, she couldn't go through a whole day without injecting herself. We were driving along in her car and Helene would have to stop and take a couple of shots because the pain was so intense she couldn't drive. She'd ask me, "Could you drive the car?" That's how bad off she was. And she felt so badly. "I'm sorry you've come all this way to visit me, Shirlè. Here I am, I can't even move."

Before I left, I told Helene she should make a serious attempt to withdraw from the painkillers. Something within me had told me to say this to her. I promised her that if she would withdraw completely, she would have a visitation.

On November 4, around 7 p.m., Helene and I had a sighting. We saw a huge light move across the sky, from east to west. It stopped just above our heads. It was then when Helene kept getting a buzzing in the back of her head. She said that she had not received anything in two years. Secretly I felt that I had come to her just in time, that if I hadn't gotten to her, the space people might pick someone else to work with me. So the buzzing in her head continued until it gave her a headache. She also noted there was some high-frequency garble. Then, much later, she received a message. We were in her car at the time, so I rushed to get a pencil, so I could write it down. The first message was as follows:

THE EAGLE THAT YOU WILL FACE WILL GIVE ME THE KEY THAT ON MY RETURN TO YOUR DWELLING WILL BRING ALL THE NECESSARY MONIES SO THAT YOU WILL TRAVEL TO YOUR NEXT DESTINATION WHICH IS YOUR NEXT MISSION.

And next, the word PERMUTATION came, and we both didn't know why or what it meant. We had someone else look the word up in the dictionary, since we didn't have one with us.

We decided it was a good word, but we still didn't understand why it was meant for us.

The next night, November 5, Helene and I went stargazing and we watched a star ride across the sky and park itself among another group of stars. Helene and I laughed. She again started to get her buzzing. She also wrote down a formula. The space people always give her formulas; it takes time for her to understand them. Then came the second message:

THE U.S. GOVERNMENT IS INVOLVED IN CHEMICAL WARFARE AND GIVEN AND SOLD TO SOME OF THE COUNTRIES IN THE MIDDLE EAST AND THERE IS GOING TO BE AN INCIDENT. IT WILL BE BY ACCIDENT. IT WILL BE USED KNOWING WHAT DAMAGE IT WILL DO. IT WILL KILL THOUSANDS—NO ESCAPE FOR MILLIONS, THOUSANDS OF PEOPLE AND ANIMALS WILL BE KILLED. THE NEGATIVE FORCES WILL BE RESPONSIBLE FOR THIS AS THE U.S. GOVERNMENT WILL BE RESPONSIBLE FOR THIS EVEN THE LEAGUE OF NATIONS SAID IT WILL NEVER BE DONE BUT THEY ARE INVOLVED AND IT WILL BE SOON.

While Helene and I were at the conference in Sedona and Steven White was channeling Ashtar, Helene suddenly poked me and said, "There's an alien standing behind Steve. He's been there ever since Steve mentioned *key*." I started writing down the message, and as soon as I finished recording what I was supposed to record, the alien simply vanished. Out of nowhere this blond alien had appeared in front of Helene, like a flash. She said, "I am sure that was for you."

Amazed, I turned to Helene. "They would go through this much trouble just for one person?" Her answer was yes, they would.

The third message came from Sedona on November 14:

THE TIME HAS COME FOR THE ONE THAT HAS BEEN CHOSEN—THEIR LEVEL OF CONSCIOUSNESS HAS REACHED THE HEIGHT TO WHICH THEY WERE CHOSEN FOR—NOW THE TIME TO ASSEMBLE HAS COME—LOOK WITHIN YOUR HEART—WITHIN YOURSELF—THE CREATOR IS WITHIN YOU THE STRENGTH TO GO ON THIS TIME OF TURBULENCE WILL

SHOW YOU THE PATH AND THE WORDS TO GATHER IN SAFETY.

Out of nowhere the word came out of my mouth ... "Permutation." Then I knew! "Helene," I cried, "I know now! The book is going to be called *Permutation*."

She said, "It's good." She paused for a while, and then out came more of the third message:

THROUGHOUT THE WORLD WE ARE ESTABLISHED OUR POINT OF CONTACT—OUR CHOSEN ONES HAS TO TURN THEIR HEADS TOWARDS THE HEAVENS AS THE COSMIC SHIPS WILL APPEAR IN GREAT NUMBERS—WILL DISPLAY SPHERES OF ENERGY TO METAMORPHOSES INTO THE BEING THEY SHOULD BE TO SPIRITUAL ELEVATION WILL REACH THE CHOSEN ONES TO UNITE THEM WITH OUR ENERGY WITH OUR CREATOR.

Then came the fourth message:

ESTABLISH YOURSELF AND THE ONE THAT YOU HAVE DIRECTED—NOW IS THE TIME TO OPEN THEIR MINDS—HEED THE WARNINGS—FOLLOW THE DIRECTIONS—CATACLYSM THAT WILL SURROUND ALL OF YOU—BEWARE OF THE FALSE OF THE PROPHETS FOR NOW IS THE TIME THERE ONES ARE COMING TO YOU TO THE LETTER THAT ARE GIVEN TO THE SPECIAL ONES THROUGHOUT THE EARTH.

The last message came over the telephone on November 18:

PROTECT YOUR LOVED ONES—AS THE TIME IS SHORT. GATHER THEM AND TELL THEM TO PROTECT THEMSELVES.

As the year 1988 drew to a close, I was home by myself one day when I heard a voice within me say, "Shirlè, sell the house." So I said out loud, "Whoever comes to the door—that is a real estate person. That person will sell our house."

Just after I finished those words there was a knock on the door. It was an agent offering me a calendar for the new year. I said to her, "Give me a call at the beginning of the new year. We will be interested in selling our home." Well, when I closed the door behind her, I began to panic a little. "What have I done?" I told myself. "I didn't speak to Fred. I'm going to get killed!"

When Fred came home, I said in a meek voice, "I did some-thing without consulting you ... don't yell at me ... promise." So I told him what I had done on impulse. I expected him to be angry with me.

"Oh, good," he said. He was glad! He said he, too, felt that we had to move.

Well, to make a long story short, we sold the house in less than a week and a half. Then we ran around looking for a new home, and we were guided to this beautiful new home. The only problem with it was its number. I decided the number of the house would not suit our well-being, because the numbers added up to five. So I paid fifty dollars to have one number on the address changed, so that the numbers would total seven. The house gave us more room and was on higher ground. I have a feeling the reason we were urged to move to higher ground is in case of an earthquake and flooding. I am afraid we are in for some unpleasant experiences.

Then, in the early hours of January 29, 1989, while we were still in our old house, I had another encounter. It was 4:30 a.m. Fred and I had been sleeping when suddenly I awoke to find two entities standing at the foot of the bed. On the left was the larger of the two beings, and I had the feeling he was male. On his right was a female. The figures appeared to be vibrating with wide stripes of red and white color which fused when they vibrated. I saw parts of red mixed up with the white. I immediately sat up in bed and they looked at me. I looked back at them, then turned around and—almost without any control—went back to sleep.

I didn't know why I had been visited by the aliens that night. At first I thought perhaps it was some kind of health checkup or warning. I thought my behavior was rather strange at the time. Why would I simply go back to sleep? Did they suggest this to me? When I telephoned Ann about this latest development, she suggested we consult Julian Joyce in an effort to find out what was happening. The following is his

January 29, 1989—The figures that appeared at the foot of the bed were red and white stripes. These colors fused when vibrating. I just saw parts of red mixed up with the white. I sat up in bed. They looked at me. I looked at them, turned around, and went back to sleep.

interpretation of my encounter:

> As for what Shirlè experienced with the two entities: This was primarily meant for her eyes only, but secondarily for all others she might contact. First, as for one being male and the other female, this gender distinction which we relate to does not exist distinctly with many space beings, only in part and only on certain occasions. We are taught that love is sex and sex is love, and we almost believe it much of the time, even when we say "a person makes loves." The basic reason for this visitation was to assure Shirlè that she is not alone and that her brothers and sisters were very interested in her present earthly performance. Shirlè is not indigenous to this planet. This visitation was also an approval statement or action from these brothers and sisters. She was not mesmerized, she rested in knowing she was doing her part and knowing her spiritual mentorship was solid. The red and white color intermingling is both a teaching and an insignia. The teaching is that spiritual healing (red) intermingles with life or God which is Life—further when we live with one or the other in major part, we live with the other. These entities have such as a principal teaching. This in major part is correct.

Two weeks after my encounter with the entities, Helene had a visitation. For the third time in her life she experienced a miraculous healing.

Always know the force is with you.

Chapter 14

The E.T.s Return

Ten days after my surprise encounter in Vancouver, Helene had an encounter in Safford, Arizona. The following is her story. It is important to note that Helene left out of this written account the things the aliens had told her about me. The reason she did this was because Helene felt she should tell me in person. Then, if I wanted to use it, I could include it in the book.

ENCOUNTER FEBRUARY 16, 1989
By Helene

I am Helene _____ of Safford, Arizona. I wish to relate my encounter of February 16, 1989, in which a miraculous healing did occur.

I am sure it was well past midnight on the above date. I was asleep and had my face turned to the wall. I was disturbed, yet not fully awake, although I seemed to feel some kind of presence in the room.

I turned over and saw the outline of something in the doorway. I turned on the lights and what I saw were two small beings in the doorway. They were small and the skin was as white as though they were never in the sun. They wore metallic suits that covered the heads, and had big eyes ... not as large as they are portrayed by a lot of people. *They in no way resembled insects.* Although they seemed not to have the muscles that humans have, I was startled and said, "Oh my God, what is this? God, you scared me!" They did smile. I did not see any teeth, but I could tell it was a smile. And I said, "I do not have any clothes on. Would you mind backing up so I can dress?"

One of them said, "We have come to help you and take away your pain, and we'd like for you to come with us. We have a shuttle waiting for you." They then backed up into the bathroom and waited until I put on my robe and sandals. And when I had put on my robe, one of them said, "Will you follow us?"

When they said they had a shuttle waiting, I expected something quite different than I saw as we went outside. I have had a healing before, in 1976, which will be briefly explained later. This ship was the same saucer type that I had been in that year. It had a soft, white glow all around it, and it could be seen clearly.

As we approached the ship, one of the beings in front of me and one behind me, they seemed to sort of glide as though their feet were not touching the ground. This was verified by many who examined the ground as my footprints showed clearly, but none were found (that had been made) by the other two beings. The circle where the ship hovered could be seen very clearly as all vegetation was dead or withered within the circle. It was hovering near the ground so low that if I had raised my hands above, upright, I could have touched it.

The beings' hands were warm and smooth as they guided me to a center of the ship, where a beam of white light came down, and I was slowly taken into the ship. The cylinder of the white light emitting from the center of the ship was six feet across and the ship itself was between 50 and 60 feet in diameter.

I was met by a tall man who looked to be six feet or more in height. He wore a gray jumpsuit and his head was uncovered. He had light brown hair and brown eyes. There was another small being with him who wore the same metallic gray as the other two. The tall man had on a gray suit, but it was not metallic as the other three small ones'. All the three small ones looked alike; I could not tell them apart. The material on the suits was very soft to handle.

I will take a little time here to explain briefly why I was in great need of help for the physical body. On September 3, 1984, an automobile accident in Las Vegas, Nevada, did a great deal of damage to my back. My vertebrae were broken, crushed and chipped. A great deal of damage had been done to the spine and a chip off one of the vertebrae had lodged in a nerve tunnel. This bone fragment was very dangerous to remove. Surgery was very expensive and could mean that I might never walk, and I had been in constant pain since that day. The pain was unbearable without pain medication.

Three weeks prior to my encounter with the extra-terrestrials, I awoke one moment to find my door ajar, but strangely enough, I was without pain. I simply could not believe it. I kept waiting for something to start hurting. I had not been free of pain since 1984. It was unbelievable but great. Within a couple of weeks of gradually reducing medication to the shot of narcotic I have taken for so long, and as all know is addictive, I am completely free of that addiction and free of all pain. I had accused Alvin, the man in a small trailer who has a key to my door, as he can answer the phone while I am out, of entering my home at night and leaving the door open. He denied this, but there is no other way it could be opened. I did ask the beings about it and was told, "Yes, we were there three weeks ago. As you were sleeping, you were taken to the shuttle and we took away the pain. But this is to remove the bone."

The morning after this happened, I called a friend and told her about it and that I had scratches on my arms and other parts of my body, like I had come in contact with a tree that had thorns. It is possible that I was floated out and did come in contact with the tree; I do not know.

He said, "We have work for you to do, and it is necessary that you be in good health." I did notice his shoes. All of them had on shoes with soles at least 1 to ¾ inches thick. I wondered about them and wondered if they were magnetic so as to cling to the deck of the ship, but I did not ask.

The small ones pulled a frame-like object out of the wall. It had four upright metal bars forming the frame and two panels across the front. They adjusted the panels to me; one breast high and the other one across the abdomen. The one across the abdomen had a box on a square object on the left side of the panel. This fit on the left side of the abdomen. I had disrobed and they placed an instrument on my back which felt warm and smooth, like the ear piece of a telephone receiver. When they exerted pressure, my abdomen began to burn on the left side where the object was attached. He used pressure in about three places on my back and I could smell burning flesh.

When I first went into the ship, there was an odor that smelled like ozone, such as one smells when you take an anode lead of a picture tube on a TV set and arc it across the picture tube.

I asked them about the burning on my abdomen and he said, "There will be a little discomfort, but it will not last long." I had no idea what could come next, and I was very nervous. My knees were shaking so badly, I wondered if I could remain standing. And he said, "Do not be nervous. We need you and want you to be in as good health as possible. We have removed the bone, but the numbness in your leg and left side is caused by spinal cord injury and we will be unable to change that."

I will give a brief description here of my 1976 contact encounter: I had terminal cancer as can be proven by the hospital records in Canada, and I had been given only a few days to live ... weeks at the most. My skin was a burnt orange and it was pancreatic cancer, which is seldom if ever cured, and I was in the advanced stage. There was no hope for me and I was prepared to die. They did work on me in the saucer-like ship and told me I would be well in three days. And I had a very bad three days. After that, no trace of cancer could be found in my body. They told me I would never have cancer again.

It is well to note that they found me again after 2,000 miles away from the first encounter. The tall one had said before he began, "The treatment that I am you—one of your other selves—as we are all one." I did not understand and wanted to know which one of us was a clone, and he said, "We are all one, connected by the heart rhythm and the brain wave. We are the heartbeat of the universe."

I felt very childlike and humble. I also felt unworthy of their trust and faith in me that I could accomplish all that they expected me to do. When I spoke of this, he said, "We think you can and we think you are, and our only reason for being here is to help you so that you may be able to do the work that was assigned to you and you will accomplish." He then gave me a container. It looked like a two-and-one-half-inch stainless tube filled with liquid, and he instructed me to drink all of it. It tasted like almonds.

I could not see what they were doing behind my back, and when I tried to look back, he said, "Remain very still. Face the front and do not move." They spoke to one another in a language I could not understand. And since I could not move, I tried to observe my surroundings.

The panel of lights was the same as I remembered them in 1976. They kept on changing and forming different patterns. There was a curved wall to the left and the frame I was in was next to the tall panel of lights; the frame was in front of the medical supply, as I call it for identification. And above it was a screen on which flashed some sort of information. I noted this when I moved out of the frame. There was also a curved wall on the right side of the panel. I suppose behind the walls were living quarters. In the center of the ship and at the top was what looked like a ruby cluster of jagged crystals hanging from the ceiling directly over and above the opening where the cylinder of light had shone. The ruby-colored crystals are enclosed in a round metal band. I asked if that was their mode of propulsion. They answered yes. There were two chairs placed to the right of the tall panel. Beneath the crystal was the opening from which we entered or floated up. The cover over the opening had been closed and it looked like panels of metal overlapping each other—disc-like pieces.

I have put on my robe and the tall one did most of the

talking. I have heard and read about the encounters in which the contactees say their people told them they were from Planet _____ and their names were _____. And, thinking I might get some information, I asked, "Where are you from?" He smiled and said, "We are from a galaxy beyond Orion." No names, no identification.

I suppose he noticed I was disappointed and said, "Do not worry, most who claim contact with us simply are not telling the truth as there are only six different species that have made themselves known to mankind, and most of the stories are not based on facts. You have nothing to worry about after your health and you will retain the numbness but will no longer be subject to the pain.

"This craft is called a shuttle, and the mother ship is larger than your largest city. It is nuclear powered. It will not be long before all of your people will see us and everyone will know what our intentions are. All nations shall be informed at the same time. All the nations that resist shall be put aside. People must know that we are here to help and to serve Earth before it is destroyed and destroys other planets along with it. The Earthlings must learn to love and trust the Creator, who is Father of all and in and through all. The degradation of Earth has been caused by religious beliefs, greed and politics and social reform. We are here to help and not harm anyone or anything. The whole of mankind must raise his consciousness as Earth people are very primitive in their beliefs and considered barbaric."

I told him I had a friend who had taken over 140 pictures of the space craft and their activity, but she says she has not seen anything—that it just shows up on the photos and that they are invisible to her eye. The same images are shown up as well. And I asked if they can, in fact, make themselves invisible. His answer was, "Some of us can, but most who say they see us do not. None of the six different species that have revealed themselves have harmed or injured anyone or anything. We are often accused of such, but it is untrue. We are often invisible to the human eye and we have been here since the first atom bomb was detonated. We are here to help, not to hurt or destroy the planet or the humans."

I asked if he would contact this friend of mine who had the pictures, and he only smiled and said, "We will be back in eight weeks."

They spoke to me in my own language and the tall one did use his mouth to phrase his words. The small ones could have been telepathic; I could not tell. It sounded in my head like I was hearing it, although I did not see their mouths move ... it is so small and slit-like. Many years ago I received an implant implanted in my head. I do receive messages, but in their language and it is extremely difficult to translate. He said, "In the future, all the messages sent to you will be in your own language and plain ... where you will be able to know and comprehend at once. This is a receiver, not a transmitter." He said, "We will help you in your laboratory, and your needs will be supplied. Instructions as to kind and type work that will be necessary is forthcoming. You will have no need to worry about money or your ability to perform."

I have every hope that I am able to create something that will help all the world and its people. As I looked at those faces and those big eyes, which were filled so full of love and kindness, I also had that feeling of love, peace and well-being. And one of them said to me, "Whatever we give is freely given, but shall not be used for personal gain, such as books ... when one person takes from another the information so that they can prosper ... often at the expense of the giver, and often the author of these books and other media sold the stories and sensationalized for the benefit of profit and the sale of this information. *Do not attract the following. This is important.*"

It is time now for us to go. Two of the small ones stepped forward and escorted me to the center of the ship. The floor slowly opened and I descended to the ground. I hurried back to wake up Alvin as I wanted someone to see the craft before it was out of sight. We got up, came outside in time to see the glow over the north mountain, and we watched it until it looked just like another star in the sky.

When I got back to my trailer, I was very happy and the clock told me it was 2:30 in the morning. It seemed like I was with them a long time, but it could have been a short time; it's hard to tell. This is as I remembered it, although I have flashes back of things that do not stick to me.

As soon as I received Helene's letter and had read it, I knew I had to fly down to visit her during that eighth week after her encounter. I needed to find out all the things the aliens had told Helene about me. I called her and she said to me, "Looks like maybe you shouldn't come because it seems they don't want a following."

So I said, "Helene, I have a feeling that I *have* to go. That's why they gave me eight weeks. I have four or five weeks or six weeks to really get this house in shape, and I'm working darn hard ... I'm almost at that stage ... and a few days for me to rest and be able to go."

"Okay," she said, "I will ask them and see if I get an answer." Several days passed and she did not get an answer.

About a week later, I got a call from her. It seems her daughter, who lives in Toronto, and has been paralyzed since a child, won a 649 star lottery of a thousand dollars. The daughter decided to go and visit her mother. Now, Helene has a tiny trailer. Her daughter didn't tell her in advance that she was coming, but told her mother to pick her up on the 9th, and here I was planning to come on the 11th.

"Shirlè, what am I going to do? There's nowhere for you to sleep."

I said, "Helene, if that's the way it is, that's the way it is ... I will try and get back my money and try to photocopy everything and send it down."

I went and tried to get back my money for my ticket, but no such deal—unless I get paid for cancellation insurance—but first I have to get a letter from Helene's doctor, declaring that she's too ill, and that's why I'm not going. That was one thing.

Next I went to a photocopier and the copies were too poor. The machine just wasn't working well. I went to two others—they were both out of order.

Meanwhile, inside something kept telling me, "You are going!" And I kept arguing with myself, "How can I be going? There's no room for me."

I came home, called Helene on the phone, and said, "Helene, I'll sleep in the lab. Just give me a blanket or a cushion, and that's it … I'm a lousy sleeper anyway. I read half the night. Just let me sleep there."

She said, "Okay, I'll arrange something. You'll sleep in the lab."

"Fine," I said.

"But," she said, "I can't pick you up in Phoenix because I'm just going to be there on the 11th, and it's over 165 miles."

I said, "Fine, is there a bus coming up?" There was. "Okay, fine, I'll make arrangements to come up by bus."

The only thing was—I would get there at noon and the bus doesn't leave until five. However, I rediscovered a cousin of mine who lives in Phoenix, and she made plans to meet me at the airport so I could be with her a few hours. Then I would get on the bus and go to Safford. But can you imagine being on the bus for five solid hours?

Six of the eight copper plates given to me by Frank.
The last two have been withheld from publication until
a future date, due to their extreme importance.

Chapter 15

Interpretation of the
Eight Plates

The week of April 11 through 18, 1989, I spent in Arizona, in a small camper next to Helene's trailer. In the week prior to my arrival, Helene suffered a traumatic setback. The space people had told her when they operated on her that her left leg would be numb, due to spinal injury, and they couldn't change that. She wasn't aware of putting her foot down and so she tripped and fractured some of her vertebrae. As a result she was in agony.

She was feeling so well after the aliens healed her. I quizzed the people who live around her and they said that she was in incredible shape. She ran, she did the most fantastic things! She even lost eight or ten pounds.

Just a couple of nights before my arrival, Helene received a message that they will come, and instead of coming with only the educational ship, they will come with the hospital ship. There was one night during my visit when we felt very strange. I thought for sure they would be coming, and I even panicked a little, although I really don't know why—but I did. Staying by myself in a little camper, I am not the bravest of souls, especially knowing there is a prison nearby. I spent every night in that camper with the door locked, because I felt sort of as though if the door were left open, I would know the aliens were there while I was sleeping. I tried to keep an alert eye and stay up all night long. As a matter of fact, I got hardly any sleep while I was there. Every now and then, when I'd start to drift off, I would catch myself.

Anyway, that night none of the dogs were barking, and as a rule, when they are around dogs do not bark. I heard nothing. There were no sounds of birds or anything at all. It was kind of eerie. I did sense that they were around. That's one thing I can always do is *feel*. Helene had said that she sensed they were there, too, and she is still hoping they will fix her back again because the three broken vertebrae hurt her so much.

Finally, on my last night at Helene's, I came to realize that they will contact me another way. Obviously, whatever I have been doing is okay. But I really desired contact with them while I was at Helene's. I guess my expectations were too intense. At least I accomplished one thing on my trip. I received the rest of my story face-to-face from Helene, and learned all the things the space people had told her about me during her February 16th encounter.

"They said that they know now that you would leave everything behind," Helene disclosed. "Now you are ready and on a higher spiritual path, and they will definitely contact you."

Asked where they came from, the aliens told Helene, "We are from Shirlè's planet." Helene then asked them if I was going to be instructed … to be taken, and the answer was yes, that they would rejuvenate me, as before. "Tell Shirlè that her work has not yet begun," they said. "The work will begin soon." In other words, my mission is a long and a lengthy one. I don't know how I feel about that, but if that's what I was trained to do from the beginning, then this is it.

I asked Helene if she is going to leave this planet or remain here, and she said, "No, that's your job. I have no teaching qualities. That is your job." Helene has her work as a chemist to perform for mankind. She knows she has a lot to learn. They told her the next fifty years were going to be important, and it seems I'm going to be here a long time if that is the case. I'll see all the New Age people and probably the Extra New Age people.

Probably the most important information Helene received from the space people was the interpretation of the eight plates that were given to me. As I mentioned before, my contact told me these were my plates. He mentioned my driver's license and medical, etc., which I take to mean were personally meant for me.

PLATE ONE

To all mankind: I have come from afar. The king has come and gone. You all of the stars and the heavens, guidance is here. The one chosen is amongst you. Many great events have taken place since the second beginning of time. You have chosen always to make war on one another. I have counted it. My brother, talk of peace. You say war. We will help one more time for this is the last time. You have the instrument of peace but you have chosen to make war with it. I am saddened.

PLATE TWO

Bless all mankind which are bound. We are related by our spirit and we are one. Our bond with other planets unites us in one image.

PLATE THREE

When all nations are at war at a time when no nations are at peace, at the end of this era will come. Major catastrophes will take place. Beware, it is the last time that mankind will be helped.

PLATE FOUR

Your mission is a long one. Youth will be given to you to help and teach all them that have been selected. The brothers and sisters who are in attendance will be told when we are coming. Beware of the false prophets that are in control of the masses. The spirit be with you.

PLATE FIVE

The knowledge, wisdom and the peace was given you. Gather your people, tell them that they are important to the survival of your species. You will be the tool to reach many.

PLATE SIX

Your rank and filing number, your date from the time of your beginning: you are acceptable by us.

PLATE SEVEN

The planet or cosmic universe where you will be waiting and instructed to be spirit, also the cosmic placement of your universe, ours are very similar, so no transformation will be made.

PLATE EIGHT

Our voice track, our methods for you to know who we are. Our followers of the cosmic rhythm, heart and brain waves are emitted the cosmic principle. The strength of the cosmic heart will follow with the principle of the universe. Your voice and heart and brain waves emit a printable pattern.

Helene was told that my personality is important to them. She uses the word *special,* but I really don't feel I am special. I do recall my contact telling me once that there were only seven and a half people in this whole universe who have the same personality as I do. I have never figured out yet what that *half* stands for. How can there be seven and a half people with my personality?

I spent one night in Safford with Helene's friend, Dorothy. She is a very kind and spiritual lady who cooked meals for us while I was visiting Helene, since Helene can't cook and there was no room for us to cook with both her daughter and myself there. Dorothy takes a lot of pictures. She lives on the edge of a vortex and sees space crafts coming and going. She simply aims her camera on her balcony and she gets strange formations, pictures of space craft and various things. Dorothy gave me two of her pictures of UFOs taken on Dorothy's roof. I actually saw two space crafts while on Dorothy's roof. We climbed up on her roof and I had a flashlight with me. I beamed a signal out to them and they beamed back. That was the highlight of my whole trip.

Photo of a space craft and space person taken by Dorothy Braatelien of Safford, Arizona. Said Dorothy: "Helene was with me when that was taken. We went in the car over past the other lake that is on the property to the west toward the mountain. She could feel them also and her heart began to palpitate at an alarming rate and we had to leave. I took this picture as we were leaving. I had told her I wouldn't go over there alone, and she offered to go with me. I knew I was not supposed to take pictures over there and I would not go alone."

When it came time to leave, I was really unhappy about having to go. Poor Helene was in such agony that she literally cried. I wanted so much for the aliens to come and help her, and I hope they do so quickly. But she did say they will contact me. I realized while in Safford that it would be in another way. That was Helene's contact. At least it did give me time to think about a lot of things.

I remember how for years I chose the material way of life. Now they know that I would walk out of my door and leave everything ... *everything*. I don't really care, it's not important. I have things because it makes me comfortable and is necessary, but it isn't my whole life. I have dedicated my whole life to the Cosmic Spirit, the One Creator. I'm glad that they have found my personality acceptable because I think the most important thing is to care—and I honestly care.

There are some fantastic people out in space who are willing to do everything to help. If you are put into a group and work to help that group achieve something, not only is it a challenge for you and what you believe in, but you are helping all those people. Actually, what else in life is there? A new dress? Another piece of jewelry? Another house? Another this? Another that? It simply isn't important. Material aspects are there because they are physical. We have certain requirements in order to survive, but when you actually put that first ... oh my God, what a waste! How much a person misses ... and the love that you can bestow on others, to open yourself completely and let the beauty flow in ... it's just beautiful.

We would exchange all this love and walk down the street, smiling, and have people actually smile back. I'll never forget a small incident that occurred recently, when I was feeling a little bit despondent (I'm human, too). I was going down an escalator and a man was coming up the escalator. He was a little bit mentally retarded—you could see that on his face. As he approached, he bent toward me and he shouted out loud, "Hello, beautiful!"

I looked at him and I perked up. I said to myself, "Here I

am the one who's always trying to do it ... and here's someone doing it for *me!*" It felt so wonderful! So always keep doing it. Say hello or smile. Just a twinkling of the eye ... something ... a recognition of the spirit. It's funny how we say, "Well, this person is a murderer," and so forth. Wrong. The spirit isn't a murderer. The body that contains the spirit, perhaps, but the spirit ... never. It's the Creator. That's why I fail to understand when people do harm to each other.

It was only recently that I found out that the shaman, Dan Whetung, is my present contact, my true agent. He is from the Greater Mississanga Ojibwa Tribe. I found that out in 1984, when he visited—projected, was taken up, or whatever—he did meet George Major from Sirius-B. George Major asked him to get in contact with me. That's how he went looking for me. I never bothered to ask him from where or what, and here he has told me that George Major was the one. He contacted me in 1985.

Dan was at the Library Outpost, which is a planet all made out of crystals and crystal tunnels. The tunnels are computer consoles made of crystal. You pull it from the wall and it works telepathically. Dan has gone with a friend on the ocean fishing. He knows things are going to start happening. There are certain things he has to do. He feels the change in the wind.

My studio

Chapter 16

Notes from Frank

Each time after I saw Frank at the shop, I would go home and write down some of the things he said. I kept a notebook of his sayings. He would only answer me if I asked the question. He never offered me information if I didn't ask for it, with the exception of what he said would happen to this planet in the future and how I was involved.

KNOW THYSELF

One thing of extreme importance that Frank told me was "Man know thyself." He felt that being true was very important. "This is an age old question," he told me, "that man should know himself, because otherwise how can he deal with anyone else if he cannot deal with himself?

"In all your searching and planning, you're still trying to understand the whole … trying not to fail to understand the whole concept." I will mention that this same message, given to me in 1972, has been brought down through the ages by various masters that have come our way. Yet we still don't seem to understand. "We are part of the same great whole of being and yet individually separate," Frank said. No two humans beings are alike.

LIVE FOR TODAY

"We prepare our bodies for the next state of being." In other words, Frank was saying whatever we do here on this planet—all the lessons we have learned—what we have accomplished—carries on into the next lifetime. Far too many people today paint an elaborate picture of the hereafter, the spirit world, the glorious rainbow land—whatever you want to call it—and they reach forward to enter into that state before they have even passed through this whole life. And they do not learn the lessons. That's why we are here, to learn the lessons. We have to live for today.

When it's time to come back, to be born again into a body, we pick our own environment from other lessons we have to learn. Life is a constant learning experience. This whole earth is a learning state. The spiritual body or soul or divinity within a person goes on into infinity. I feel people are mistaken when they cling to their religion and say to one another, "Let's die because we're going to bask in God's glory." You can bask in God's glory if you want to, but sooner or later you have to fulfill the mission.

You become the Creator and prepare the environment in which you will journey. Only when the environment has been prepared, then it is the right time to go forward and to leave behind the physical. We are here for a purpose and it is essential that we learn every lesson. Rather than run away from different experiences, we need to go forward and live these experiences. "Gather into your being the light of the spirit, the light of understanding," said Frank, "and then peace comes from within."

GOLD FOR PROTECTION

There is an entry in my notebook dated January 16, 1972, early morning: "The disc pretty … partly awake in a semi-state. I was given a gold disc and I only saw a strange hand. I accepted the disc with this knowledge. I asked my friend the meaning of this gold disc as it is very large, and his answer was 'From now on you must always wear gold at all times. It is for your protection against the negative forces.'" To this day I wear gold.

ON MEDITATION

Frank talked about imagination. "Never limit yourself," he said. "What travels in the imagination in time then becomes reality, for the present reality is still an idea, and the life you are living is only a mental one. The world is only an idea in your mind." He told me I should go into my painting and there I would find my reality.

I once asked Frank about meditation. He said, "As an artist, or anybody who is absorbed in his work, you are really meditating." He told me I didn't have to meditate, but if it made me feel good, well then, of course I should meditate. "But being so absorbed in what you're doing, you are meditating. You leave the other world and in this state you are in contact with the inner world. It takes you away from the material world and then turns your mind inward. Anyone in this profound state, whether it's a world situation or spirituality, is really practicing meditation."

The point he was trying to make is that people who feel it is essential to meditate, or people who want to meditate and cannot, need not worry so much about it. They are doing it anyway. I'm not saying all meditation is wrong—quite the contrary. But if you're doing it in a way, such as writing, music, art, or you are absorbed in what you do, you are actually practicing meditation. I was glad to hear about that because I find I cannot meditate for long, perhaps four or five minutes at a time. I simply have a hard time doing it.

WHEN THE TIME IS RIGHT ...

Frank said, "There is only one consciousness. One light shines through the human being and the light is divine. Everything in this universe has its appropriate place. Every event has its appropriate hour." In other words, we all have our own timing. Until reviewing these notes for this book, I never realized what he actually meant. Your particular timing is your time. Whatever you are doing has its own timing. You may work hard getting things done in the manner you desire. That has its own timing. Eventually you work all your life through this to get what you want to achieve, and that is the timing. I realize now, too, that the whole miracle of life is timing.

Sometimes you throw a question out to space and you can't find the answer. But when the time is right, you will get that answer. Everything is answerable. That's why there is a time to live, a time to die. That, to me, is a whole miracle of life.

LOVE AND HATE

Love, of course, is the highest expression of life. It comes from understanding, not from emotions or sentiments, but from within. Love comes from within us because we all have this divine essence. It's too bad a lot of people do not choose to use this love. Instead they choose to use all-consuming hate. If hate is in a person, that's what they are going to give you. If you've got love, then that is what you're going to give.

Frank mentioned once about people hurting me. He said if they were to hurt me, I should not worry about it, because of the law of cause and effect. Whoever might hurt me would simply be hurting himself. What goes around comes around— the karmic rule. I find it interesting that so many people do not realize this.

Love is the most important thing in life. Through love all the good vibrations are coming from this love that you are generating, allowing the light to circulate from yourself to others. Hate, on the other hand, is like a black heart that cannot penetrate. People with love simply have to love. That's the only way, because their spirits speak through love.

TRUTH, THE ESSENCE OF LIFE

"Truth is the most important thing," Frank said. "The only way we can help mankind is through truth. The truth does not mean your concept. There is only one truth of everything. It's true that every human being has their own concept of truth, but when they say, 'I think that what you're doing is stupid and rotten,' that's not truth. People think that is their truth. They have to learn to allow people to breathe and do their own thing.

"The truth is that love exists; unfortunately, hate also exists. Going by way of expressing and loving and giving displays truth, the essence of what life is about—to know yourself."

Frank said, "Ask these three questions: What am I doing here? What's it all about? Where am I going?" He said, "These are the things that keep on generating the person to search for their quest of where and how they will express themselves. Expression is their truth."

CENTER OF THE COSMIC SCHEME

So many people have gotten killed because they have tried to help humanity. There have been all these mystics who sort of had a small opening into the universal mind and tried to help people, to get them to search for their quest. Very few have been accepted. And it's always a very few, right down through history—the few that change the world. It's these few that makes you feel, 'Thank God, this life is beautiful.'

"We all have to work inwardly and outwardly to try to bring the world to the Golden Age," Frank told me. "Man is at the center of the cosmic scheme. It's too bad so many people are not ready for the higher vibrations." Frank always felt there were so few people who will be ready for the higher vibrations.

An example comes to mind. We had a man visiting us who would have nothing to do with UFOs. At the same time I had Aileen Edwards, Ron Chaput and Michael Ross as guests who were sleeping over on a Saturday night. Naturally, the subject of UFOs was bound to come up, and here was this friend visiting from Australia, who put a strain on the weekend. Talk about walking on eggs and trying not to upset anybody! He did such a terrible job of upsetting everybody that it nearly drove us crazy.

Actually, I believe this was another test for me, to see how I would handle this situation. There will probably be times when I'll be on the road, giving lectures and so forth, and I'll have to deal with a lot of skeptics. I just hope I don't have another experience like that weekend.

SEX AND MARRIAGE

Frank talked about marriage and the love between a man and a woman. "The most important thing when a man falls in love with a woman is that he is able to look beyond her physical nature. He has to ask himself, 'Can I live with this person? What about her mind? Is she interested in many things?' Most people don't take this into consideration. They fall head over heels in love, and when things don't work out, it's because they don't have anything in common. Sex is wonderful—it's an expression—but it isn't the essence of a relationship."

FOOD AND POSSESSIONS

My contact was philosophical about many things, including food. He said not to "eat too much because it makes the body coarse and heavy. And eating too little makes the body crave food. You have to eat moderately, never to excess."

As far as material things are concerned, he said, "You can have all the beautiful things, the richness of material life, but do not be possessed by these things." He said you can have everything you can, if it's your destiny to have them. "But know one thing. If you've got to leave at a moment's notice, just put the key in the lock and walk out." Can you do that? There are probably many people who cannot. How unfortunate for some of the Jews in Germany during World War II, who when they knew things were going to happen, couldn't leave their possessions. And so they died with their possessions. What people should understand is that possessions are possessions, which can be replaced. But your life and everything that you hold dear within yourself is simply too precious to be lost.

WE ARE HERE TO HELP

Describing his race, Frank explained that they are "the higher beings and have placed ourselves to watch over mankind. We will still try to save mankind. We are here to help." I know that my friend and six others who were involved with him did try. That is why he contacted various people he thought could help.

I want to help with my entire being, because I believe in this whole process. Through millenniums, in other worlds and other times, there were people involved in helping. It was always the few that were helpful and in turn were helped to rise and enter a higher dimension.

The masses have always been around. There are always going to be so many people who simply are not going to make it. Here we are back in the same state, another civilization in trouble, and again just a certain amount are going to make it. The others will not. But I feel if we help these people, then it's possible that in their next lifetime they will be better off. Then we can at least say that we tried.

TEACH THE TRUTH

"If you meet people who are searching for the truth and are ready for the understanding, then you have to teach them the truth," Frank said in 1973. "You are compelled to do so." So this is it. When people come up to me and ask questions, this is my mission.

It's so important to be spiritual. I have to mention that here is where some of our UFO researchers go astray. While they are dedicated scientists of ufology, many of them simply do not understand the spiritual aspect. It's the spirituality in a person that is most important.

THE FORCE IS DESTINY

"Man is also a creator and is creating his own world—of expression, of experiences, truths—and is aware of a Force ... and the Force is destiny." Frank went on to say that "Man maps out his own light, is creator of his own fate, good or bad. Some people learn from suffering rather than from pleasure.

"Destiny, which you have earned in former lives, is working out now in this lifetime. If you find peace within yourself, no one can take that away from you. You have found light eternal. Know that you are the temple of the living God."

CLOSED EARS

Whenever we discussed in the store anything that had to do with space aliens, I noticed all the customers walking around. A little worried, once I said to Frank, "They're listening."

He just looked at the crowd, then turned to me. "They will not hear this. They are not ready to hear us."

I realize now that when you want to tell somebody something, if someone is not ready for it, they will not hear you. They're not going to hear anything you've got to say.

INSPIRATION CAN MOVE MOUNTAINS

One time he said in passing, "The planets that are nearer to the physical sun have beings that are more evolved than ours. Those planets that are more distant from the sun are less evolved. The intelligence on some planets may not be human in our sense, yet they are individuals far ahead of us in understanding and spirituality. They do feel a lot of compassion for Planet Earth and are ready to help people who are involved and searching for the essence of life. The wonderful telepathic communication throughout the universe comes from the one Cosmic Mind. And no distance, no matter how great, can stop it.

"Although man works with invisible forces, he finds a blazing trail which leads always upwards toward the light." In other words, if he wants the help, it's there for him. "Everyone has gifts that have been given to them, but the greatest gift is inspiration. With inspiration we have the desire to move mountains."

SOME PREDICTIONS

I will include some of the more startling things Frank told me. "There are space bases on the dark side of the moon, where spaceships land from many planets in the galaxy. There are souls from worlds in space that are crying to be born on Earth, as Earth is one great big classroom, and we all get our experiences from here. There is no law that says we ever have to come back. We can remain in eternal paradise. We don't have to return to physical life if we have earned it. We have all eternity to do it."

He spoke of the natural catastrophes that will occur. "The places or safe areas or countries that won't really be hurt by it are some parts of Canada, Australia, New Zealand and part of the United States, such as Colorado, Utah, Arizona and New Mexico. The Four Corners will remain. The polar ice caps will melt."

Frank made the comment, "Everybody wants to call this new age *their* new age." Going on, he disclosed that the western portion of America, the greater portion of Japan will go into the sea. "Europe will also change. There will be upheaval in the Arctic and Antarctic, eruption of volcanoes, the shifting of the poles. The Eastern Coast (New York, etc.) will go into the sea. So will the western part." He said it will happen in my lifetime.

CROSSING DIMENSIONS

"The flesh cannot travel to the stars," said Frank, "but your art will carry you there. Do everything as well as you can. Be careful of assumptions. Assume nothing."

He told me to stand by a few and he gave me a number, but I prefer not to mention the number. He said only a very few would cross over to the fifth dimension.

I was also told that there is a tunnel in Denmark which is a time-travel tunnel to other dimensions.

RELIGION AND SPIRITUALITY

"Religion pulls people apart. Spirituality brings them together." Frank said the word spirituality actually means physicality of the heart—"of the understanding and the love and the truth, of knowing that every human being belongs to the whole, and to feel and understand the other person. Never condemn or assume unless you walk in that person's shoes or until you go through what that person has gone through."

Sure, we all make mistakes. There are always two

different roads to take, and we don't always choose the right road or the easy way. Sometimes we take the more physical road and expect to have physical things. But we do grow and develop. As a consequence, if we learn more of our lessons on this plane, it becomes more likely that we don't have to return. And that's wonderful.

But people do seem to have a wrong conception of what it's like—to sit in front of God's feet and play the harp. Can you imagine what that would be like—sitting and listening to the harp all day long? It's the most stupid concept of what life is like in the hereafter.

The important thing is we have to live now, each moment, because every moment is different. That's the beauty of it. You can walk around with love in your heart. You can walk down the street and people are going to smile at you because you are really smiling from within. You don't have to smile from your lips when you're smiling from within. That's what's important.

When I knew him those two years, I always thought Frank would be there for me. Maybe I should have written more things down about what he said, or taken a photograph of him. I just assumed he would always be there for me.

Actually, I feel he still is. Sitting on the couch, for instance, I will all of a sudden feel something turn me around. That's when I know he is there. When I'm having difficulty, he stands by me. He has never let me down.

AFTER WORD

It has taken us four years to get this book into print. A lot has happened and continues to happen. By no means is this the end of the story. The saga is still going on, and perhaps one day will be told, for we are approaching sooner than we think the time when all of this will come together.

S.K.C. and A.C.U.

Creation

With brush in hand
the artist strokes
the living canvas
of her hopes
and dreams
and wishes
to compare
her living work
with Laylah's hair.
"Oh why the World
in wonder be
like this easel
on my knee
of listening
and seeing too
a universe
of A and B
in me and you!
With vivid light
and darkness pair
the seen and unseen
ordinaire
with nature's bent
the obvious-maximus
is meant
and yet the shadow
plays the real event!
Burnt ochre speaks
of Druidic fires
in forests green
beyond empires
of steel
and glass
scarring skies
of parks and places
put aside.

The canvas cloaks
the brush conceals
the living thought
the heart reveals
in absence
silently
it strokes
in brilliant color
drunken boats!
The woman's hand
it holds the key
the gate will open
inwardly
the artist paints
the message clear
it's in your eye
then in your ear
of listening.
Open to the brush's flare
bathe in whisps
of Laylah's hair
and enter there
in visual words
another universe
of no compare
anywhere but
here and now.

Pan/3/8/90
Frank Lewis Morton

I have a Grandma came from outer space
She's a pretty gal with a happy face
She doesn't belong in the human race,
But she knows someday she will find her place.

She's a funky lady from way out there
Beyond the moon and the sun, behind the dragon's lair
The only thing that changes is the colour of her hair
Someday she's moving on, and then you'd best beware.

>   CHORUS: Grandma, Grandma
>   Come out and play
>   I want to see
>   The stars today
>   Grandma, Grandma
>   How much can you see
>   From your great big ship
>   On the astral sea?

What is that
Up there in the sky
Not a bird, not a plane.
But it sure can fly
With a sparkling laugh
And a twinkling eye
You know it's my Grandma
Come from way up high.

>   Grandma, Grandma
>   Come out and play
>   I want to see
>   The stars today
>   Grandma, Grandma
>   How much can you see
>   From your great big ship
>   On the astral sea?

Bubby, this song is as yet untitled and unaccompanied. As soon as the song is completed, you will be the very first to hear it. I love you.   —*Heidi*

(My grandchild wrote this song at the age of 15.)

THE AUTHORS

Shirlè Klein-Carsh completed her fine arts studies at Sir George Williams University (now Concordia University) in Montreal, Quebec. She completed a course of studies at the Museum of Fine Arts, Montreal, under Dr. Arthur Lismer (one of the Canadian Group of Seven Artists). She also studied at the School of Fine Arts, Saidye Bronfman Centre, in Montreal. She has exhibited her art in many places over the years, in Montreal, Vancouver, Australia, Paris, the Soviet Union, New York, California, as well as Surrey, B.C. and Nelson, B.C. "Art is what comes from within unyielding in its demands," she says. "I try to bring to my personal philosophy a deep vision and a determination to use accumulative mastery of form and color to depict important spiritual values." You can view paintings at Shirlè's Web site: **http://nsartists.ca/shirlekleincarsh**.

Ann Carol Ulrich received her B.A. in Creative Writing from Michigan State University. She has published short stories in children's and adults' magazines, features in newspapers, and is the author of The Space Trilogy (*Intimate Abduction, Return To Terra* and *The Light Being*), along with several romantic suspense novels under the name Ann Ulrich Miller, including *Rainbow Majesty* for light workers. Her spiritual autobiography, *Throughout All Time, A Cosmic Love Story* tells about the life she shared with her husband and soul mate, who passed away in 2008. Since 1987 she has published a metaphysical newsletter, *The Star Beacon,* through Earth Star Publications (**www.earthstarpublications.com**).

Made in the USA
Charleston, SC
04 September 2013